CUNARD
150 GLORIOUS YEARS

CUNARD
150 GLORIOUS YEARS

John Maxtone-Graham

DAVID & CHARLES
Newton Abbot   London

Previous page: John Young's
painting of RMS *Queen Mary*
at Southampton. It is sunset
and the forward hold is opened
as cargo or mail is being loaded
on board for the run to New
York. (*John Young*)

Illustrations from the Author's Collection unless credited otherwise.
Thanks are also due to Royle for the loan of a selection of pictures
reproduced in this volume.

British Library Cataloguing in Publication Data
Maxtone-Graham, John
   Cunard: 150 glorious years.
   1. Great Britain. Shipping services: Cunard Line,
   history
   I. Title
   387.5′06541

   ISBN 0-7153-9344-8

First published 1989
Second impression 1990

© John Maxtone-Graham 1989

Book design by Les Dominey
Typeset in Bembo and Bodoni by
Typesetters (Birmingham) Ltd
and printed in West Germany
by Mohndruck GmbH
Origination by Columbia Offset

for David & Charles plc
Brunel House   Newton Abbot   Devon

CONTENTS

INTRODUCTION

This 150th birthday is more than a significant Cunard milestone: it is the first decimal birthday that the company has been able to celebrate appropriately since 1890. That year, the Cunard Line was fifty years old; there was a banquet in the home port and encomiums in Liverpool, London and New York newspapers that hailed the first 'Jubilee of the Company'. *Etruria* and *Umbria* were in service, *Campania* and *Lucania* were anticipated in the decade to come.

A quarter-century later it was 1915, and in the turmoil of World War I the anniversary passed with almost no notice. There was a post-war substitute celebration in 1920, the Line's eightieth anniversary. That year, a banquet was held in the first-class dining saloon of the newly acquired *Imperator* (soon to be *Berengaria*), moored in Liverpool's Gladstone Dock.

The hundredth birthday fell on 4 July 1940, the first grim summer of World War II. There was neither the time nor the inclination to celebrate anything; France had just fallen and most of the British Expeditionary Force had been evacuated from Dunkirk. Both *Queen Mary* and *Queen Elizabeth* had been requisitioned for war service.

But even for this peacetime birthday, there are complications. The Japanese have chartered *Queen Elizabeth 2* for portions of two successive years, starting in 1989 and including 1990; on 4 July of that sesquicentennial year, Cunard's flagship will be on her way home from Yokohama. She has often called at the port during world cruises, as did *Franconia* and *Caronia*, drawing record crowds every time. All Japan, it seems, is in love with her, embodiment of those glistening, ingenious gadgets that the Japanese, adults no less than children, so enjoy. At stationers in every Japanese port, where cards and calendars are sold, chances are that representations of *QE2*'s familiar profile will be available.

But she will be back on the North Atlantic, just after the anniversary day, in mid-July of 1990, sailing eastbound from New York en route home from Japan. Then she will make a special tour of historic Cunard ports in home waters, including Cobh, Gourock and Liverpool, after which there is to be a review of the fleet in Southampton. Then, just as the little *Britannia* did 150 years ago, *Queen Elizabeth 2* will set her course west from England to North America. She will sail from Southampton instead of Liverpool, she will embark hundreds rather than *Britannia*'s dozens, and her destination will be New York rather than Halifax and Boston. And the sense of completion that marks the end of every voyage will be especially sweet that summer morning in New York harbour; Cunard will have completed a century and a half of extraordinary service binding old world and new in peace and war.

Several Cunard histories have been published over the years and, for that reason, I have chosen to make this one different. Strictly speaking, it is not a history at all; readers will find no chronological, sequential development from past to present. Rather, I have chosen to detail aspects of Cunard vessels and crews customarily unexplored. We will examine the vagaries of early decks and saloons, recount the life of a steward who led a strike on the *Mauretania* but rose to become one of *QE2*'s restaurant managers, share circumnavigation of the globe on one of history's most comfortable cruise ships and see how troops sailed to the

Crimean and South African wars on board early Cunarders.

Bermudian painter Stephen Card has created a beautiful cover, a symbolic encounter at sea between Cunard's first and present flagships; my thanks to him for generously donating it to New York's Ocean Liner Museum. Peter Radmore deserves especial thanks for putting his marvellous Cunard collection at my disposal. I was most cordially received by the staff who look after Cunard's archives at the University of Liverpool. Thankfully, yet again, Norman Morse's encyclopaedic knowledge of transatlantic deck plans has proved invaluable.

Additionally, I am indebted to the following, listed alphabetically: Adrian Allan, Susan Alpert, William Archibald, Joyce Beer, Alan Bennell, Joseph Brandt, Sir Hugh Casson, Geoffrey Coughtrey, Bernard Crisp, William Donnell, Eric Flounders, Sheridan H. Garth, Erling Johannessen, Ronald S. Keats, Daria Kelley, Lorayne Killingley, Dennis Lennon, Harry MacDonald, Paul Mason, Victor Millar, Lynne Naylor, Jonathan Norton, Andrea Owens, Stephen Payne, Ron Santangelo,

James Stacey, Peter Wheeler, Ray Williams and Clare Wright.

And surely a final paean of thanks is due to Trafalgar House who, in 1971, took charge of Cunard and restored the company to its rightful pre-eminence. Historically, the name Trafalgar has been synonymous with triumph; in terms of Cunard, it still is.

Having looked backward, it is tempting to look forward as well, to Cunard's bicentennial. How will the company's fleet list read in July 2040? It would not surprise me if a fourth Queen-class vessel were in service by then, perhaps the *Queen Diana*; how intriguing to know how she will look, how she will be powered and how she will compare with her trio of illustrious predecessors. But there are many sea miles to sail before then and so, to all Cunard masters, officers and crew, and to all passengers who sail in their care, this sesquicentennial volume is respectfully dedicated. God speed!

John Maxtone-Graham
New York City, 1988

WELCOME
Aboard

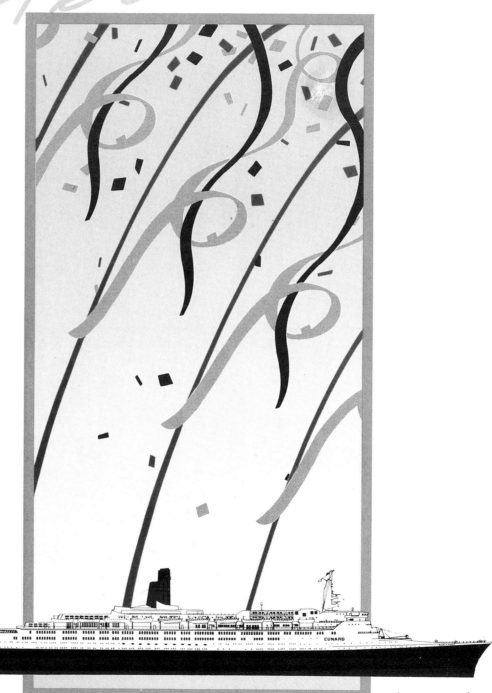

A menu cover from the QE2.

Some of your Lordships now sitting here will live to see steamships crossing the Atlantic.

The Earl of Stanhope in the House of Lords, 1793

. . . and will, during the continuance of this contract, diligently, faithfully and to the satisfaction of the said Commissioners for the time being and with all possible speed, convey Her Majesty's mails and dispatches twice in every month from Liverpool.

Excerpt from Cunard's Admiralty Mail Contract of 1840

Early on Saturday morning, 29 April 1865, there was an impromptu meeting of the Cunard Line's board of directors. The anxious men gathered in the company's Liverpool boardroom at 8 Water Street. Waiting outside in the ante-room, his face contorted with grief, was the company's senior marine superintendent. News of Sir Samuel's death had arrived from London the night before. The morning papers were full of it, so full in fact that first detailed reports from America of President Lincoln's assassination were crowded off the front pages. The hastily convened directors were debating whether to delay the sailing of the *Asia* as a mark of respect. But after a bleak discussion, they concluded unanimously that postponing in any way the departure of a Cunarder was the last thing their so recently deceased founder would have wished. The marine superintendent was summoned and instructed to have the *Asia* sail on schedule. After all, what would Sir Samuel have said?

The 'steam lion' was gone. Cunard, founder of an extraordinary transatlantic institution, had died peacefully in his seventy-eighth year, surrounded by sorrowing family and servants in the bedroom of his house in Queen's Gate Gardens. Earlier that same day, through his son Edward, he had dictated a conciliatory letter to his old but estranged colleague George Burns: '. . . this is the last message, I fear, you will ever receive from him'. There had been time for a final communion and, at six in the evening, Sir Samuel had breathed his last.

He left behind a phenomenally successful company, then in its twenty-fifth year. His fleet of crack liners, which had started as a quartet of modest steam packets in 1840, had doubled in size within ten years and, by the time of the founder's death a quarter of a century later, had weathered all storms, commercial as well as meteorological, to achieve maritime immortality.

The family's origins had been German, the name anglicized by Sir Samuel's immigrant grandfather from Kunders to Cunard when he settled in Philadelphia. The name still resonates in the public consciousness; it is said that, to the man in the street, mention of the name Cunard evokes greater shipping recognition than any other. Not necessarily so in Paris between the wars. An American, anxious to reach the company's office in the Rue Scribe, ordered a cab to take him to Cunard. The driver looked blank. Finally, after repeated admonitions of 'Cunard! Cunard!', he hurtled his frustrated passenger into the Bois and pulled up with a squeal of brakes next to a duck pond. 'Voilà, monsieur,' the baffled taximan exclaimed, 'voilà vos canards!'

The Cunards were Tory sympathisers and, during the American revolution, they abandoned Philadelphia for Halifax where second generation Abraham Cunard found work as a dockyard car-

penter. His son Samuel was born in 1787. He grew
up a paragon, blessed with archetypal Victorian
attributes – caution, wisdom and thrift. Never one
to waste a moment, he used to drive the family cow
out to pasture knitting a sock as he walked in the
beast's wake. Once his schooling was complete, he
too took a post at the dockyard, apprenticed, not
surprisingly, in the engineering shop.

Later, both Cunards forsook employment to
establish A. Cunard & Son, a coastal shipping line.
They christened their first vessel the *White Oak* and
their earliest trade routes were confined to the St
Lawrence, upriver to Quebec. Despite a severe
Halifax depression, the business prospered; Cunard
& Son's vessels ranged as far out into the Atlantic
as Bermuda or southwest to Boston. In 1815,
Samuel married Susan Duffus. She presented him
with eight children before she died thirteen years
later. In addition to attending to a demanding
business, Samuel Cunard had to raise his large
family single-handedly. But he did well. In 1820,
when he bought his parents a retirement farm, he
changed the company name to S. Cunard &
Company. His fleet numbered forty vessels,
cornerstone of an empire.

Contemporaries described him as 'a small grey-
haired man of quiet manners and not overflowing
speech', but a man, according to an envious
colleague, who 'made both men and things bend to
his will'. Another recalled that Cunard boasted a
'brisk step, quick and ready movements', never
quicker than one summer evening of 1838 at John
Brown's house in Hollis Street. Cunard was dancing a quadrille when a bomb was hurled through
the front door. Disregarding the danger, he
stamped out the fuse and threw the bomb back into
the street; there, it exploded, shattering every

E. D. WALKER

window in the house and knocking Samuel and his dancing partner to the floor beneath a deluge of falling plaster. But, thanks to Cunard's 'quick and ready movements', no one was hurt.

His business caution was legendary. In 1829, he responded to a fellow Canadian who had written proposing that their two companies establish a line of steamers:

We are entirely unacquainted with the cost of a steamboat and would not like to embark on a business of which we are quite ignorant. We must, therefore, decline taking any part in the one you propose setting up. Your humble servant, Samuel Cunard.

But within a decade, on his own behalf, he bent the marine steam engine as well as the Admiralty to his will; the westbound departure of *Britannia* on 4 July 1840, marked the inauguration of not only the first steam service but also the most famous name in Atlantic history.

It is irresistible to speculate on how Cunard might have reacted to development within his company during the century and a quarter following his death. Even before he died, Cunard's steamers no longer had the North Atlantic steamship service to themselves. During the 1850s he had seen the Collins Line, an American enterprise designed specifically to thwart his Atlantic mastery, fall by the wayside, victim of questionable seamanship and bad luck. But by the time of his death in 1865, Hamburg-Amerika Linie ships had been sailing to New York for nine years, the French Line's *Washington* for two. His great British rival, the White Star Line, had not yet entered the transatlantic lists and no Holland-Amerika Linie

vessels would sail out of Rotterdam for another eight years.

When Cunard died, his last great paddle-steamers, *Persia* and *Scotia*, were popular but outmoded company flagships. The vastly more efficient propeller was overdue; Samuel Cunard had, in the words of one amateur historian, 'stuck with paddles too long'. What miracles those propellers would achieve! Alas, Sir Samuel knew none of them. Would that his lifespan had paralleled that of little Willie Heatherington who, as a Liverpudlian boy of ten, had watched *Britannia* sail on her maiden voyage. Sixty-seven years later, as an old gentleman, Willie marvelled as *Lusitania* steamed out of the same Mersey for New York. And yet *Lusitania* and her sister, *Mauretania*, were only the first of a staggering new breed of Cunard superliners.

Cunard from the beginning had been primarily concerned with the passage of mails; indeed, passengers were not even mentioned in his original mail contract. The safe and efficient delivery of mail had been and would remain the linchpin of his company's service. It was an arduous service, not without problems. Early masters' reports convey, in stark brevity, the nagging vulnerability of those first Cunarders. *Britannia* seems consistently to have been the unluckiest. '*Britannia* delayed on the homebound passage in consequence of having damaged her forefoot in Halifax during a fog, went to Saint John, New Brunswick, for repairs.' On another occasion, *Britannia* had to 'put back, rudder-head twisted; *Acadia* took on the mails'. Other entries state that '*Britannia* delayed two and half days on the homeward voyage, having struck Cape Race and went to St John's, Newfoundland, for repairs' and '*Britannia* detained on the outward voyage 36 hours having grounded on Cape Cod'. Sister ships suffered as well: 'Columbia arrived April 20th, one engine only working, the other damaged.' Columbia would 'break her back on the American rocks' in 1843, to be replaced by Hibernia and 'flying Cambria'. Groundings, defective engines and appalling North Atlantic weather were doubly prohibitive since Cunard's Admiralty contract spelled out stiff fines for delays of any kind.

But the precious mails, stuffed in four-foot canvas bags originally called portmanteaus, reached port; even more important, safety and reliability emerged as imperishable assets of Cunard's 'tin kettles'. Stevenson Blackwood, secretary of the General Post Office, later spoke warmly at a luncheon celebrating Etruria's launch. Between 1840 and 1884, he announced proudly, 'the Cunard Line has carried 17,000,000 letters without the loss of a single mail bag'. Staggering as that record seemed, the late Sir Samuel could never have guessed at the increasing volume his ships would carry in years to come. During 1929, 633,099 mail bags were loaded; since each contained approximately 2,500 letters, the total for that year alone was over 15,000,000.

On a typical westbound arrival, Aquitania

RMS Campania *at the Liverpool Landing Stage. She and her sister,* Lucania, *were the last word in transatlantic speed and style in the 1890s, a vision that the founder would not live to enjoy.*

steamed into New York harbour carrying 6,000 mail bags. Although earlier Cunarders had had to deliver their mail to the Manhattan post office, now they were met at Quarantine by a trio of US Postal Service mail boats. Largest was New York harbour's postal flagship, *President*; she could carry 3,000 mail bags, her smaller consorts only 1,500 each. They tied up along either side of the giant Cunarder in prearranged order; letters destined for the United States, Central and South America would be off-loaded to starboard, those for Canada, Mexico, China, Japan and Australia to port.

As soon as long canvas mail chutes had been suspended over the ship's sides, *Aquitania*'s crewmen began hurling mail bags as fast as they could – fifty bags a minute – down to the boats. (At the other end of the run, *Mauretania* crewmen in 1925 had unloaded 3,600 mail bags at Plymouth in under an hour, a record rate adopted as the company norm.) In New York, unloading the *Aquitania* became an unofficial fortnightly contest between Cunard crews above and their US postal colleagues below, the Britishers trying to overwhelm the Americans, the Americans struggling to clear away mail bags that threatened to clog the bottom of the chutes. Sometimes, the friction of cascading portmanteaus whizzing down caused a chute to catch fire.

Whenever one of New York's notorious harbour fogs enveloped the anchored *Aquitania*, she remained immobilised until it lifted; but the determined mail boats cast off regardless, radioing ahead to the sorting station on Pier 72 as they groped upriver through the murk. On more than one occasion, *Aquitania* mail arrived as far west as Cleveland before exasperated, fog-bound *Aquitania*

Oil painting of Samuel Cunard currently in the offices of Cunard Ellerman. (Cunard)

passengers had disembarked at Pier 54. So too, eastbound mail destined for London in the twenties arrived there via crack Great Western express trains from Plymouth (locomotive *Shooting Star*) long before *Aquitania* had been eased into her Southampton berth.

Whatever the delays encountered by westbound mail, knowledgeable New Yorkers had a way of getting even faster delivery to Great Britain. They would come to Cunard's New York pier and slip packets of letters (and a tip) to the pier's waiting-room steward. He would pass the letters on to friends on board the next express liner to sail who would stamp them and slip them into a Fishguard or Liverpool postbox while the mail bags were still being unloaded from the hold.

What would Sir Samuel have thought, had he known that a novel communication net, faster than his beloved mails, would link his vessels not only with either shore but with each other as well by the turn of the century? A Cunarder was not the first transatlantic liner to be equipped with Marconi's wireless; that honour went to *Lake Champlain* of the old Beaver Line. Then the ships of the North German Lloyd followed suit. It was not until the next year, 1901, that *Lucania* had a Marconi set and wireless operator on board, first used on the 15 June sailing. The *Campania*'s was fitted three months later so that when the two ships passed in mid-ocean, they enjoyed 140 miles of continuous communication. Bereft of sails, their dual pole masts sported wireless antennae instead.

One impecunious young American put Signor Marconi's invention to instant good use that autumn. His name was Henry Robertson and he was travelling westbound on *Campania*, very short of funds. But salvation lay just over the horizon.

15

His mother, he knew, was booked on the east-bound *Lucania*. As the two Cunarders steamed within range, a signal crackled from *Campania*:

Mrs J. L. Robertson passenger Lucania pay purser Lucania £10 asking him to advise purser Campania pay me Love Henry.

Perhaps from long force of habit, Robertson *mère* caved in. Within a quarter of an hour, crackling through the North Atlantic ether, came a response couched in formal cablese:

Purser Graham Campania pay Henry Robertson £10 have collected £10 from his mother aboard Lucania, Purser Milliken.

Solvency was thus re-established, courtesy of an indulgent mama, two co-operative Cunard pursers and Marconi's sublime apparatus.

Cunard passengers no longer travelled in a blind limbo for a week. Marconi's new invention saved lives as well as allowed publication of the *Cunard Daily Bulletin* in 1903. Sir Samuel would have been amazed had he known that his mid-ocean passengers could now follow stock markets in New York or London, keep track of elections and, most rewarding for new transatlantic papas, be advised of the sex and weight of babies born in their absence.

In June 1841, Cunard had received a confidential letter from James Campbell of the General Post Office. Cunard's first four steamers had been in service between Liverpool, Halifax and Boston for nearly a year. The letter began 'My dear Cunard' and ended 'have you ever seriously thought of the port of New York as your point in the States instead of Boston? This quite *entre nous*.' The actual

move was made six years later. But that early change involved only the western terminus; what would Sir Samuel have said had he known that after World War I, the company's express service would abandon Liverpool for more convenient and competitive Southampton?

Would Sir Samuel ever have believed that, at the same time, his vessels would be fuelled by oil instead of coal? Or that during a fearful depression ten years later, some of his company's most prestigious tonnage would be withdrawn from the Atlantic to steam idly around the Mediterranean, Baltic or Caribbean, booked by curious throngs for their first cruises? What could he have made of the aeroplanes that, starting in 1939, unleashed a victorious airborne assault on all ocean liners, leading to the latters' demise within three convulsive decades?

Sir Samuel was knighted by a grateful Queen Victoria after he had delivered his vessels with, an admiring colleague commented, 'no haggle of price nor driving a good bargain for the company' for trooping service to the Crimea. Seventy-five years after his death, undreamed-of giant Cunarders would embark 15,000 soldiers – an entire infantry division – racing them across a hostile Atlantic at over 30 knots.

And what would Sir Samuel make of the present day, 150 years after *Britannia* chuffed out of Liverpool for the first time? He would not, presumably, be surprised to find that a Cunarder, the company's flagship, was the fastest vessel in service; but it would sober him that she was unique, the world's last express liner. Harder still would it be to absorb the radical change in today's shipboard, with its almost total dependence on cruising. And would he not be astonished to find that, of Cunard's present seven-ship fleet, four sailed originally under Norwegian colours? He might well be amused that two identical contemporary luxurious Cunarders accommodate exactly the same number of passengers as *Britannia*.

And would it not amaze and perhaps mystify the company's founder that millions were boarding vessels each year for the fun of it, that they were not actually going anywhere but were booking for a holiday instead? How extraordinary, Sir Samuel would muse, that most late-twentieth-century passengers confine themselves cheerfully for weeks or even months within cabins on board white-painted hulls with slab sides, open decks, swimming baths, casinos and indoor amphitheatres, deriving pleasure rather than peril from their sea voyage.

It astonishes me – and I wonder if Sir Samuel would even approve – that I can breakfast in bed so comfortably on board *QE2* in the middle of an obstreperous North Atlantic. While I read the ship's newspaper (no longer, alas, the *Cunard Daily Bulletin*) with my toast, the adjacent sea-sound through the portholes is reduced to a faint, regular mutter as the sea miles surge past. The cabin's television reproduces in miniature the view ahead. A remote camera, focussed forward from the bridge, provides a splendid visual counterpart to the music on an accompanying track. Whatever the selection played under that heroic scene, whether the deft progression of a Bach suite or the overripe sonority of a Brahms symphony, it suits the picture exquisitely. As *Queen Elizabeth 2*'s prow thrusts effortlessly through the worst the Atlantic can offer, the music serves as triumphant and reassuring accompaniment. Once again, I cannot help wondering 'what would Sir Samuel have said?'

A menu from Queen Elizabeth 2.

17

When I was on the *Mauretania* in 1963, the ship was running between Naples and New York . . . The ship had very heavy competition from the Italian Line vessels *Galileo* and *Italia* and was fighting a losing battle, but I met many Americans who told me that they always travelled by Cunarders, as they had a soft spot for that line.

William Harvey, a retired steward.

What Sir Samuel established in addition to his thriving fleet were indestructible links between Britain and the United States. It was not until 1909 that Sir Evelyn Wrench and Walter Hinds Page had their historic, exploratory conversation that would flower, post World War I, into the English-Speaking Union. Yet their joint perception – that Americans in England 'should be made to feel at home' and vice versa for Englishmen in the US – had, in a very real sense, been pre-empted by Cunard. For by then, the company had long since created its own transatlantic club. Cunard fitted eastbound Americans like a glove and, throughout the company's first century, Americans by the thousand were 'made to feel at home' repeatedly in the cosy, glistening fastness of Cunard cabins.

Whatever impulses dictate a passenger's choice of vessel were as critical for the Atlantic ferry as they are in today's highly competitive cruise market. In those crossing days, timing was much more crucial. One had to disembark in England or the United States in time for a meeting; cruise passengers have merely to be home before Monday. Yet, then as now, establishing and sustaining unswerving

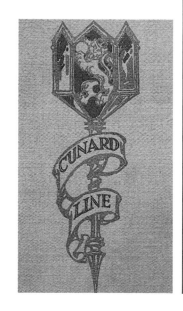

A sampling of Cunard covers from the 1890s to the 1920s. (Peter Radmore Collection)

One of millions of baggage tags affixed to Cunard luggage over a century and a half. This tag of Mrs Ogilvy's memorialises her last round trip on the second Mauretania. It bears the now defunct U.S. Customs sticker as well. (C. Stanley Ogilvy)

Queen Mary sailing from New York, 1937: Even from afar, a sense of anticipation and excitement pervades the crowded decks. Americans throng the giant Cunarder as always and the man silhouetted against the bridge screen waving his hat typifies the mood of a prewar New York sailing. The traffic light atop Pier 92 has turned green, permitting the Mary to enter the river. (Photograph by Paul Hollister)

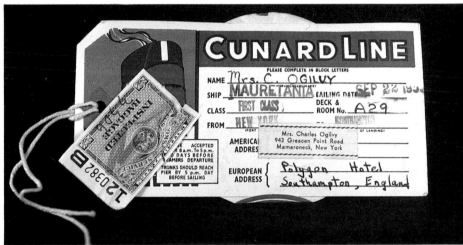

passenger allegiance was shipping's *sine qua non*. And, although divining the prospective passenger psyche was a bewildering and aggravating task, Cunard brought to that wooing game certain undeniable advantages.

For those bound on commerce, their ships were fastest; for those fearful of storms, their ships were safest; for those crossing for the first time, their ships were peculiarly hospitable. A British ship and, by extension, a British landfall, appealed to neophyte voyagers; insular, stable and understandable Britain served as a welcoming European threshold. Indeed, England seemed the ideal stopping-off place where Yankees could get their touring feet wet before coping with the rascality, real or imagined, of incomprehensible 'foreigners' awaiting them on the continent. If you booked and boarded the Cunard in New York, Boston or Montreal before World War I, your first destination was inevitably the United Kingdom. For, until the transfer of their express service to Southampton in the 1920s, Cunarders touched at no French port en route to Liverpool; Cherbourg did not appear in company brochures until the 1920s.

On board summertime Cunarders sailing out of

New York towards the turn of the century, a new mood suffused the vessel, adventurous anticipation supplanting immigrant angst. The crossing as pleasure had arrived, the crossing as ordeal was over. The almighty dollar booked cabins eastbound as well as westbound; unlike immigrants, American families embarking for a grand tour sailed both ways. Cunard beckoned and, once booked, every member of those families adopted the company as his or her own. After all, the founder himself had been a transplanted colonial and seemed especially

19

qualified to cater to his North American cousins. Perhaps his secret was that the Cunard Line, although staunchly British, seemed somehow gregariously American as well, its appeal weighting evenly both sides of the transatlantic scale. That special American focus remains a company strength to the present day and one is not surprised to find that Cunard's largest office is located neither in London nor Southampton but in New York, at the western terminus of the ancient route.

Historically, the bonds between American passengers and the English crew they met on board have always been strong. Predictably, for those venturing abroad for the first time, it was infinitely reassuring that the vessel on which they heaved out of the Narrows was manned by men and women who spoke more or less their tongue. Trays would be delivered, deck chairs rented, money changed, cables dispatched and dishes brought to the table in a slightly unfamiliar but comforting English.

And that initial Cunard appeal might never end. Passengers who had crossed happily once tended to continue doing so; moreover, a pervasive company allegiance spread throughout the land by word of mouth from one contented client to another. Young Cunard passengers – who under two years of age had travelled free – would, as adults, book cabins with the same company that their parents had always used.

Testimonials from devoted American passengers tell the tale. To quote from a letter from the late Vieva Perrin:

I remember so well my childhood and early youth on those magnificent Cunarders. My mother would only go on the Cunard Line, as they 'never lost a life'. We went so often on the

(Below) *The American impact on Cunard vessels. The Long Island Phipps family had embarked in strength for the westbound crossing of* Mauretania *in the mid-twenties.* (From *Halcyon Days* by Peggie Phipps Boegner and Richard Gachot)

(Right) *A busy sailing day from Manhattan's super piers in the fall of 1952. Four Cunard White Star vessels dominate the foreground:* Media, Mauretania, Queen Elizabeth *and* Georgic; *behind them stretch* Liberté, United States *and* Conte Biancamano. (U.S. Coast Guard Photo)

WHEN THE PHIPPS FAMILY CAME STEAMING HOME ON THE LINER MAURETANIA.

Caronia (the old *Caronia*, that is) because it was named after a schoolmate, Caro Brown, whose grandfather was Mr Vernon H. Brown, New York agent for Cunard Line; she and her parents went, so we went too . . . My most exciting trip was the *Mauretania* in September of 1908 when we met a hurricane. One of the propellers broke and we drifted in the trough of the sea, the masts snapping like whips in the wind and the waves

(Right) *Painting of RMS
Aquitania by Hayao Nogami*

Leaves from the Aquitania's
*launch booklet. Perhaps the
apotheosis of the engraver/
printer's art, this last great
Cunarder to appear before World
War I was accompanied by reams
of the most elegant publicity
material, as though the larger the
vessel, the more ambitious the
ephemera connected with it.*
(Peter Radmore Collection)

mountainous, each one torn by little ridges, like sand in the desert.

Mrs Perrin's crossings started in 1905 on *Campania* and ended with *Queen Mary* sixty years later. Until 1910, she was booked exclusively with Cunard but then, perhaps seduced by the size and luxury of the new White Star ships, her parents switched eastbound to *Adriatic* (but home on the *Lusitania*), then *Oceanic* (home on the *Caronia*), then *Olympic* (aborted by collision with HMS *Hawke* in September 1911). In the twenties and thirties, Mrs Perrin experimented with Italian and Dutch ships but always alternating with a salting of Cunarders like *Berengaria* and, once again, her beloved old *Caronia*. After World War II she invariably sailed on the Queens or the second *Mauretania*. Throughout her long passenger life, Cunard retained a firm hold on her affection.

Elinore Marvel recalled:

We originally sailed on the Holland-America Line as my father was the physician in the US for the Diamond Workers Guild . . . Later, we were Cunarders [interesting usage of the word to encompass passengers rather than steamers] and all three of the pre-World War II ships were as familiar to us (and my husband in the late twenties and thirties) as our own home.

She also wrote 'perhaps the ship I know best for a most peculiar reason was the *Aquitania*'. Mrs Marvel and her husband were stranded at Ambrose Light by impenetrable fog on board *Franconia*, en route home from the Caribbean in December 1929. That involuntary Ambrose stay was dry, since it was the era of prohibition and they were deemed

inside the 3-mile limit, and lasted for two wearisome days. To pass the time, Mrs Marvel completed a jigsaw puzzle of the *Aquitania* that she found in the deserted second-class lounge. 'On my next crossing on her, I could have found my way around blindfolded.'

Incidentally, Mrs Marvel completes her *Franconia* memoir with an evocative maritime moment when the fog finally lifted:

> An unforgettable sight met our eyes. On either side of us, as far as one could see, the transatlantic fleet was lined up. They were all carrying Christmas mails and Christmas passengers, so there was an unusual number of them: *Aquitania, Berengaria, Ile de France* and a flotilla of lesser ships.

In some early Cunard sailing schedules, listed along with the dates and times of departure was the name of each ship's master, a reminder to former passengers that an old friend would be the host for their crossing: come and sail with Captain Pritchard again. In the days of the long New York turnaround, grateful New York passengers had every opportunity to fête their favourite master; a group of them once gathered at Delmonico's to present Captain Lott of the *Persia* with 'an elegant set of silver plate'.

An anonymous couplet circulated by the company in the late-nineteenth century described the archetypal Cunard master to perfection: 'A man of middle age/In aspect manly, grave, and sage.' It was a description lost on one young American lady passenger who boarded *Mauretania* in 1924 with her Irish setter. She summoned the first uniformed man she saw, mistaking him for the ship's butcher, and asked him to take careful charge of her pet. The man, gravely and sagely, took the creature's leash and promised to do his best. Once the girl had departed, Captain Arthur Rostron turned the animal over to a subordinate.

That Cunard passenger/crew symbiosis worked both ways. An American woman recorded: 'Particularly delightful in memory, the marvelous Cunard service. For instance, the deck steward on the *QE2* who, as he tucked in my steamer rug, said: "Madam, I remember you from the *Mauretania*." Imagine being remembered by a deck steward who meets thousands!'

Anne Smith had the most poignant recollection, not only about Cunarders but about one of the company's servants as well:

My first crossing was in 1912, on the old *Carmania* and I was seasick every creaking night for ten days. My [first] husband, Charles V. Mills, was lost on the *Lusitania*. He was on a short business trip to Belfast and I did not go with him. I was twenty-six and only four years married.

I remember the first report of the tragedy [which] said that everybody was saved and my family and friends gathered around that evening and we all joked that he had probably lost all his luggage. My husband was a strong swimmer and so fond of children that I always thought he would have helped them if he could – he was undoubtedly at lunch.

Out of the despair of her husband's final crossing, Mrs Smith clutched at a comforting thought from his letter written on board just before sailing, the last she would ever receive:

On our *Carmania* trip in 1912, we had had such a nice table steward named Le Touzle; my

Crossing's end: Tugs push Queen Elizabeth's *bow into Manhattan's Pier 90 and, dressed for disembarkation, American passengers throng the Promenade Deck. Their cabins are empty and already made up for their eastbound successors.* (Tug photograph by Paul Hollister)

husband wrote me that the first person he saw after boarding the *Lusitania* was Le Touzle, so he undoubtedly sat at his table. Le Touzle was lost too and I have always regretted that I did not write to Mrs Le Touzle in England.

I attended the memorial service at St John's Cathedral several Sundays later and I shall never forget the boy soprano who sang 'Peace I leave with you, my peace I give unto you' – it was heartbreaking on top of all.

In 1986, C. Stanley Ogilvy found in his attic a baggage label still fastened to a suitcase. He says:

Although the date is not clear, this represents my mother's last transatlantic trip in September of 1959. She died the following month. Indeed, she was so ill that we did not want her to try it, but we knew it would only make her even more ill if we tried to stop her.

That is one reason why I am sure it was 1959. She normally went up to London and elsewhere to visit friends. But she was an anglophile, and also loved the *Mauretania* and the *Aquitania* and just wanted to make one more trip to England. So she lodged at a hotel in Southampton for a few days and came right back, perhaps again on the *Mauretania*, I don't know.

That potent Cunard affection continued, in Mrs Ogilvy's case, to the very end; like so many of her generation, she was a Cunardophile.

The company saw to it that appropriate promotional literature anticipated the crossing. Just after the turn of the century especially, and long before the advent of colour film, Cunard pamphlets and brochures rejoiced in richly embossed covers,

Getting the message to the passengers: Cunard's brochure covers hinted at the elegance and refinement on board their magnificent trio, in service prior to World War I. (Peter Radmore Collection)

(Right) A Lusitania *menu with a superb embossed view of the vessel above it.*

increasing elegance of Cunard brochures peaked with *Aquitania*'s launch booklet of 1914 with its heroic title page, decorative margins and effusive prose. Each page of text was bordered within a luxuriant jungle of intertwined acanthus, dolphin and, lurking in ambush at each corner, chaste naiads, their classic innocence sullied with a hint of forthright, nubile prurience. It was all in perfect good taste – lavish Edwardian-style indulgence overlaid with a wink. What made that brochure and others like it significant was their attempt to elevate the crossing into a kind of architectural experience. Similarly, that concern for rich elaboration reflected Cunard's determination to equal or outdo the threatening elegance of rival *Olympic*-class tonnage no less than the overbearing Hamburg-Amerika giants from across the North Sea.

So Cunard's message reached American clients via ingrained company loyalty, efficient word of mouth or pretentiously stunning brochures. In every passenger home, as the frisson of sailing day approached, all the promised elegance and practicality of Cunard's steam service was reduced to a prosaic sheaf of papers – tickets, letters of credit, passport and inoculation certificate – as well as a mountainous accumulation in the front hall. There were piled brass-bound steamer trunks, valises, satchels, strapped portmanteaus, steamer chair, steamer rugs, camp stool and, for lady passengers, less a hat box than a hat trunk.

From the hinterland, the sea voyage began with a railed preamble, a jolting, dusty journey by train to Grand Central station followed by a preparatory night or two in a Manhattan hotel and a giddy whirl of urban glitter and shopping on embarkation eve. Perhaps most sorely missing from contemporary travel abroad is that marvellous, anticipatory

multi-coloured inks and extravagant design. This new sophistication suited Cunard's newest offerings; only the most elaborate art and typography could do justice to superliners *Lusitania* and *Mauretania*. (What a far cry from the founder's original spartan intent! Splendour rather than safety seemed the subliminal message now.)

A few years later, *Aquitania*'s vaulted Louis Seize interiors demanded even more ambitious reproduction on an even grander printed page. Indeed, the

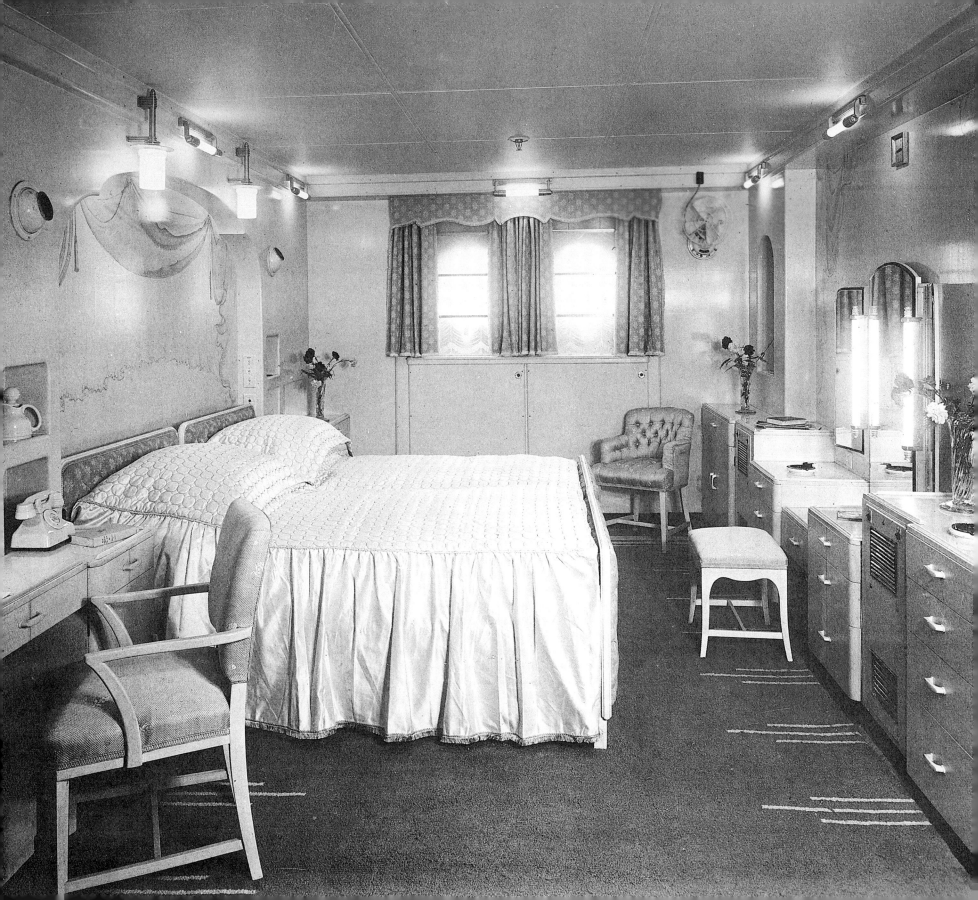

progression to sea; air travel has wiped that slate ruthlessly clean. In the old days, Cunard passengers experienced a deliberate, step-by-step achievement from home to station to hotel to pier, increments of excitement now encapsulated within one grace-less hurtle from home to airport. Occupants of today's jets may dismiss that sequential, pre-crossing travel as time wasted; but, curiously, one word that seldom appeared in steamer passengers' diaries was boredom, a term regrettably endemic to flight.

Westbound passengers relished the same prepara-tory ritual, savouring the cumulative stages of their journey – rungs up the ship's sides, so to speak –

that have no equivalent in the throughwayed impersonality of all our airports. All that New York lacked, nay, never needed, was the boat train that after three hours from London to Liverpool deposited Cunard's westbound passenger within girdered Riverside station adjacent to the landing stage. Here coal smoke from locomotive and funnel formed a pungent amalgam in the sooty, suddenly salted air of the Mersey.

Passengers boarding in New York approached the pier by hired two-wheeler or carriage, rattling through Manhattan's grimy dockside sprawl. Their destination was the industrial Italianate façade of steamship company offices separating 12th Avenue

A typical First Class cabin on board the Queens.

Prior to the twentieth century, Cunarders tied up and passengers embarked and disembarked through these portals. North German Lloyd is just to the north. (New York Department of Ports and Terminals)

from the Hudson River. New York piers, unlike their European counterparts at the opposite end of the run, boasted no cranes; so early Cunard steamers tied up almost concealed from the adjacent cobbles. Only the tips of the mast betrayed the vessels' presence, as well as acrid hints of coal smoke and a pervasive tidal reek.

Gathered from a spectrum of American states, hundreds of alien travellers (strangers now but fellow passengers by dusk) inched seaward through a clatter of hooves and iron-shod wheels, jockeying for kerb space with sweating draymen delivering cargo and last-minute mail. Deposited on the pavement, passengers surrendered their luggage as well as over-generous tips to piratical porters. That passenger tide flooded through the pier building towards the vessel. There, flow was constricted again as tickets produced from wallets or reticules were scrutinised by Cunard staff and checked against the neat, inked columns of the company's booking ledgers. Past that final hurdle, the pas-

sengers started up the gangplank.

The older docks were as low as the older ships. The original finger piers ringing Manhattan were simple, merely a pile-girdered platform rising feet above highwater mark. The gangplank's gentle slope achieved *Umbria*'s strength deck so that symbolic transfer from shore to ship was simple and direct; passengers strode onto the vessel's open deck. Having achieved the vessel, their next direction of travel was down below to find their cabins.

Later, as taller Cunard hulls towered over the water, the piers accommodating them grew taller too. Gangplanks could no longer reach main-deck railings so passengers boarded, perforce, through openings nearer the water. Naval architects pierced hull plating with double-doored ports the size of bank vaults that led into embarkation lobbies far from sunlight and air. Henceforth, from *Carmania* right up to *Queen Elizabeth 2*, every Cunard passenger would pass, as Sir Hugh Casson has said, directly 'into the veneer-lined belly of his new home'.

Brand-new Mauretania *steams down the Tyne. Painting by T. Henry.* (Cunard)

The arrival of Lusitania *and* Mauretania *in 1907 necessitated a move uptown to 16th Street and Pier 56. Cunard ships* *berthed there until the* Queen Mary's *arrival in 1936.* (New York Department of Ports and Terminals)

Inside Pier 92, one of Manhattan's three super-piers, 1,100ft long – plain, pedestrian structures that were stifling in summer and freezing in winter. (New York Department of Ports and Terminals)

On board at last, that passenger pilgrimage was concluded along the soft electric glow of panelled corridor, down alleyway to port or starboard and into the stateroom at last. There, they were welcomed by respectful if distracted white-jacketed stewards and, just as likely, the shrill greeting of visitors who always seemed to have embarked and inspected the vessel long before their passenger hosts.

Forgive those newly boarded passengers now if, having achieved their objective, they cannot merely sit and talk. The restless sea urge is on them; they can manage no more than a distraught euphoria. Embarkation anxieties preoccupy them: 'Where's the small black bag?' 'Look under the bunk, are both steamer trunks there?' (They always were, miraculously, strapped, locked, having been unseen for a week.) A sudden panic, 'Are you sure you have the keys?' and then, 'I must ring for the steward, we need another vase.'

Husbands are dispatched to reconnoitre the dining saloon: 'My dear, do see that we are seated at the purser's table; he knows we're on board.' Scarcely out of the door, another request: 'Don't forget to cable Mama. And on your way back, please stop by the writing room for some letter paper, there are all those thank-you notes.' Missions accomplished, husbands return with several stiff, cream-coloured sheets, each bearing its authoritative, engraved 'At sea onboard RMS *Campania*'. 'No, there's no need for you to mail them, I shan't be done before you leave. The pilot will take them off.' Those same letters, franked 'Paquebot Mail' would arrive at their destination the following day, the sender already remote.

But first they must be written and the spirited cabin conversation languishes. Visitors fall silent and fidget, relieved, abruptly, when the steward's gong is heard in the corridor or an impatient blast of the ship's whistle shakes the cabin. Then, such embraces, followed by a rush to the embarkation lobby and more embraces. Visitors crowd wistfully onto the gangplank and, interspersed with knots of port officials and shore staff, disembark onto the strangely deserted pier.

That is the final arbitrary separation – those who sail and those who stay. Some visitors extend their vigil to the very last, gathered at pier's end and waving until the faces at the rail can no longer be distinguished. The pier has its own magic, second only to the ship's. An outbound passenger remembers 'the smell and atmosphere of Pier 90'. And that, by its very number, was a memory from the thirties or after, when the 1,000ft (305m) Cunarders – Cunard White Star tonnage now – discharged and received passengers at mid-town, farther upriver than old Pier 54.

But, in truth, it made little difference whether boarding *Umbria, Campania, Caronia, Mauretania, Aquitania, Berengaria* or any of the Queens; that embarkation ritual remained unchanged, regardless of the vessel's size, a ritual sustained to the present. For, such is the mystical shipboard continuum, what our parents and grandparents, as well as their parents and grandparents, did on board ships, we do too. And Cunard has been part of that exhilarating process for a century and a half, embarking and accommodating generations of peripatetic Americans bound for abroad.

And what, finally, of the passengers? They had finished their letters, unpacked that portion of their luggage needed on board, eaten their first Cunard lunch and, suddenly, blissfully idle, with book and steamer rug in hand, sought out the deck steward.

Out on Berengaria's *open deck in the 1920s: an unknown lady passenger takes her ease at the ship's rail. Stout walking shoes, a quizzing glass and cigarettes complete her on-deck kit. (The University Archives, The University of Liverpool)*

After dinner it commenced to rain and I began the long walk of the deck, at which I was engaged when Tea was served. This meal consisted of tea, toast and crackers, at eight, after which I resumed my promenade until two bells when I journalised and went to bed.

Diary excerpt, John Merritt, eastbound, the *Washington*, 1864

Gorgeous morning. Lay in sun, then along to First. In sun again in afternoon. Tea with Miss Usher. Horse racing at night.

Diary excerpt, Ethel Pidgeon, westbound, *Queen Elizabeth*, October 1946

More than anything, transatlantic passengers confined below decks on early sailing ships craved fresh air and light. Too often, they were denied both; either the sea was too rough or the open decks untenable because seamen and the sails had first priority. The introduction of steam reduced the need for canvas, resulting in expanded deckspace. A new generation of grateful passengers liberated from cabin and saloon discovered that, in addition to fresh air and light, they craved exercise as well, a means of walking off Cunard's substantial transatlantic fare.

So, of all the uses to which an ocean liner's decks have ever been put, whether shuffleboard, deck tennis or, more recently, swimming and sunbathing, it was extensive and vigorous walking that mattered most. Passengers rejoiced in any opportunity to exchange the foetid 'tween-deck atmosphere for lungfuls of that tonic restorative, sea air.

The long, broad vista of Queen Mary's *capacious Promenade Deck. The pattern of sun-struck windows leaves its distinctive mark along the teak.*

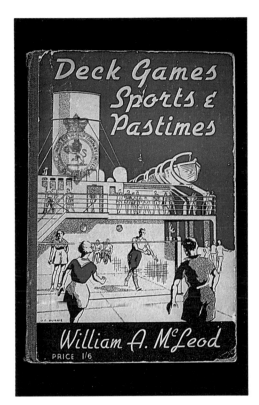

A company publication designed to cover every passenger amusement out on deck save one – sleeping in a deck chair. (Peter Radmore Collection)

Queen Mary's bellboy corps out on deck for a group photograph with the Second Steward. The man in the front row is the uniform designer. (Queen Mary Historical Archives)

But, on board every vessel right up to the present, an obligatory ritual precedes every walk, a deck ceremonial to which passengers of every ilk have always fallen prey. Venturing outdoors for the first time, they all lean over the nearest rail and gaze at – what? In mid-ocean, nothing, nothing, that is, save the heaving Atlantic. Nevertheless, they carefully survey the horizon, scrutinise the waves, peer aft at the wake or, screwing their heads around, make sure that the funnels are still in place.

Granted, occasionally there is something to be seen. A Cunard passenger in 1898 remembered: 'When word came from the lookout up in the crow's nest, or even from a passenger at the railing "Whale ho!" we all crowded around to see a long black shape. Generally, we would see it spouting.'

But whales were rare and one Cunard master confessed ruefully 'I am tempted sometimes to pass off dolphins as whales'. Preoccupation with other ships was traditional for, in earlier transatlantic times, passing vessels might be called upon for assistance, provisions or merely the latest news. 'Spoke a French vessel at four o'clock', recorded one nineteenth-century passenger diarist, indicating that both ships had slowed and stopped while their masters exchanged east/west bulletins by speaking trumpet.

But if, as usual, there is nothing to be seen from the rail, no whale or porpoise or ship, other passengers, binoculars at the ready, are always ready to fill one in. Doubtless the popularity of present-day cruising may be partially explained by

The inviting, wind-swept expanse of Mauretania's *Boat Deck in mid-ocean, as irresistible for determined walkers as the Matterhorn for mountain climbers. The picture was taken before 1912 because of the scant number of lifeboats.*

ships by the half-moon sponsons that protected the thrashing paddles.

Save for the tallest, a view of the sea was unlikely. So little height separated open deck from often menacing sea level that substantial bulwarks were essential to provide precious additional feet of freeboard. Sometimes, even those protective bulwarks were ineffectual, as in a stormy situation on board the little *Batavia* of 1872 under Captain Moreland:

By four o'clock, the sea was running very high. At half past seven, our starboard bulwarks were stove in and the water entered the main saloon. At a late hour, the hatchway on the port side came in with a crash and the sea following flooded many of the staterooms on that side.

The number of Cunard decks increased from one to two on board the *Scotia* of 1862. The vessel's strength deck still ran the length of the hull from stem to taffrail, but along both of *Scotia*'s flanks were sunken alleyways, open to the skies but still protected from the sea by high bulwarks. Only the upper deck boasted railings of the kind with which we are familiar today. That surrounding trench of promenade deck permitted passengers an unobstructed, if narrow, encircling walkway more or less their own.

the Caribbean's frequency of islands, other cruise ships or small craft; there is invariably something to see at sea on a cruise, a vista woefully deficient during crossings.

Cunard's naval architects did not always smooth the compulsive walker's path. Whereas, on later Cunarders, four or five unobstructed circuits added up to a brisk mile, decks on the first sailing steamers were less salubrious. They offered promenading passengers a cluttered progression at best, less a promenade than a gritty tour of a ship at sea. There was only one outdoor level and that alpha and omega of deck accommodated every soul on board, working or walking: seamen, bakers, cooks, officers, off-duty stokers and sometimes livestock, all crammed together and further obstructed amid-

QE2 passengers in their deck chairs, sleeping, sunning, gossiping and reading.

immediate visual access to the sea. Canvas awnings could be unrolled from above and below, creating a damp tunnel for those determined on fresh air regardless of dirty weather. (Never underestimate the walker's dedication: one fellow passenger on board *QE2* during a winter crossing confessed that she did her deck laps way down on 4-Deck, achieving her daily miles indoors along cabin passageways, only occasionally obstructed by stewards hoovering the carpet.)

Gallia was followed by *Etruria* and *Umbria* and they in turn by Cunard's crack 1890's pair, *Campania* and *Lucania*. These two 'last words in ocean liner design' would be eclipsed after the turn of the century by 'the pretty sisters' *Carmania* and *Caronia*; they would be successively dwarfed by *Lusitania, Mauretania, Aquitania* and finally the Queens.

It was curious that with every advantage that should have accrued from their gargantuan hulls, *Mary*'s and *Elizabeth*'s designers opted not only for no shelter deck at all but very different promenades as well. Both Queens' promenade decks were only quasi-outdoor, teak expanses that never got wet so that even coco-matting runners were unnecessary. They were permanently lined with deck chairs, head inboard, with a view through sometimes misted, occasionally open but always protective glass. Those promenade-deck windows on the Queens could only be opened by a deck steward, providing during fine or humid days near New York a sheltered approximation of open decks.

Incidentally, that promenade-deck gentrification on the first two Queens was significant, yet another insulating step away from the sea. On board *Queen Elizabeth 2*, there is no promenade deck whatsoever: flanking deckspace has been incorporated withindoors. The entertainment lounges run the

It was not until Cunard's *Gallia* of the 1880s that historians mark the emergence of the modern steamer's deck configuration. The *Scotia*'s trench was widened on the new ship, its walls withdrawn inboard. The trench walk had become the strength deck while the former main deck served now as roof of the central deckhouse. Bulwarks were gone and a railed, partially covered walkway offered full width of the vessel. Only outside the library and card room on quarter-deck's port side amidships is there a fragment of traditional promenade deck, but it is carpeted and its original deck chairs have been replaced with sofas facing the sea.

A sheltered view of the sea on board Cunard's present flagship is possible but not through a traditional promenade-deck window. Symbolically, the company and hence the passengers they carry are more involved with the vessel's interior than the elements surrounding it; life on board this last transatlantic liner is largely a self-contained, interior experience. Somehow the ocean, no longer a spectacle in itself, counts for less.

On board *Queen Mary*, walking passengers had two contrasting circumnavigational paths at their disposal: indoors on the promenade deck or, one flight up, outdoors on the boat deck. Walking within that echoing, stuffy promenade deck was a far cry from the gusty alternative above. And whereas a stroll round the former might well be interrupted by an encounter with deck-chaired friends en route, there was scant chance of that in the bracing semi-gale lashing the boat deck. It was there that the serious walkers gathered each morning, upholstered against the wind, determined to achieve several sea miles before lunch. The deck, still damp from either rain, spray or a matutinal scrub, stretched invitingly ahead. On most transatlantic days, the ship would be pitching rhythmically so that juxtaposed deck and horizon lines contracted and expanded like some devilish concertina.

Which direction to walk, clockwise or counter? A study has ascertained that people lost in Canada's forested wilderness bear almost imperceptibly but unerringly to the right, ultimately achieving a great

Coastal cruising's delight. Sun-capped mountains seen from a deck chair.

circle that returns them to their point of origin. Apparently, deck walkers succumb to the same impulse, invariably setting out from starboard exits towards the stern, circling the vessel clockwise, veering, as in the Canadian wilds, instinctively to the right.

Of course, a few aberrant walkers always pursued a reciprocal, anti-clockwise course, posing

39

for themselves as well as for those they encountered a ticklish socio-maritime dilemma: how – and how often – to greet? Passengers circling the deck in opposite directions meet each other twice on each circuit. How to react on each successive passage – to speak or not to speak, to speak once and then nod, then smile, then finally ignore? Crewmen have the solution; passed on deck, they deliver one breezy 'Good morning!' and no more. A second is superfluous, a third ludicrous. And all this olla-podrida before the first mile has even been logged!

On nearly every Cunarder, completing a ship's circuit around the bow was never easy. (There is a cautionary sign, DANGER HIGH WINDS, posted permanently below both port and starboard staircases ascending the observation crescent just below QE2's bridge.) The vortex of confusing winds that ravages the forward curve of every deckhouse raises havoc with even the most determined circuit-maker. But true walking aficionados persevere regardless. The vessel's normal headwind intensifies within range of that forward deckhouse curve, escalating from Force 1 to Force 6 within a few paces. Walkers slow and hunker down into an almost foetal crouch, maintaining as low a profile as possible against the blast while negotiating the turn. The wind's onslaught is such that headscarves and trouser legs ripple uncontrollably; unless held firmly atop the head, hats tend to be dislodged.

Just around that corner, overlooking the plunging bow, there is a curious windless hiatus, the eye of the walker's storm, all the more remarkable for the typhoon that has just preceded it. It lasts only an instant. Continuing over to starboard, one's back catches the wind, just as unnerving, indeed, almost elevating. Shoved aft precipitously, walkers spread their arms instinctively for possible support,

Tea in a deck chair, a mid-ocean delight. Note the little brass frame on the left-hand chair-back that identifies the occupant for that crossing. (Right) *Shuffleboard on board* Aquitania. *The numbers have been chalked rather than painted on the teak.* (Far right) *A captain at play, dragooned by passengers on a Cunard cruise into some sort of deck game. Top and far right pictures,* The University Archives, The University of Liverpool)

only increasing the gale's manic purchase. Bowled along, one flies on tiptoe across the teak. Encountering oncoming walkers while rounding those curves is comical, a bizarre contrast of walking styles: one is crouched and plodding, the other almost flying out of control, Willy Loman meets Mary Poppins. But within seconds, the tempest drops as the straightaway is achieved, and the clockwise walker continues aft unhindered, sailing before the wind, reaching around the stern before tacking strenuously up the port side again.

When the first steamer chairs (that was their original name) appeared, walkers inevitably ran foul of them in their path – colonies of chairs where sedentary fellow passengers shrouded in rugs took their air supine. One cannot blame them; steamer chairs have always offered a seductive deck alternative. When God turned His hand to furniture, He perfected the steamer chair first. If not necessarily

soft, it remains essentially right. There is something divinely inspired about the slope of the back, the incline of the seat and the elevated ease of the footrest; the occupant is cradled more soporifically than in any seating ashore. No matter how bracing the air, how intriguing the conversation, how gripping the novel, after only minutes in a steamer chair, the passenger inevitably succumbs to an irresistible maritime torpor, sinking into a somnolent recumbency.

The first Cunard passengers made do with no deck seating whatsoever. With the working of the sails, there was no room to install seats of any kind; only later were park benches bolted to the deck. But resourceful passengers brought their own chairs from home with them. Collapsed, folded, lashed and tagged, these came on board with the trunks and were consigned by stewards into the damp gloom of deck lockers. Once the crossing

What to do in a deck chair on QE2: Sunning (with Spitzbergen in the background), sleeping, staying warm, reading (alone or en masse) and (facing page, lower right) the author enjoying tea on board the only ship left in the world where it is delivered to your chair by an obliging deck steward.

began, seamen or energetic male passengers would retrieve them and set them in whatever protected space could be found along deckhouse walls. Gyrating vessels came equipped with wooden slots to keep steamer-chair legs in place. Compulsive deck sitters – every bit as dedicated as walkers – had their chairs lashed to adjacent deckhouse railings, regardless of the weather. There they remained, even throughout appalling storms, often intruding into the path of the walkers.

Indeed, sitters and walkers skirmished unendingly over territorial rights, sitters disturbed as walkers trooped past, walkers obstructed as they pursued their circuits. (Yet a third warring deck element would arrive with shuffleboard.) But a solution was achieved, first on board a non-Cunarder, the *City of Rome.* Her broader promenade deck was subdivided – outboard Rotten Row, inboard maritime seating. Walkers and sitters were formally separated so that both open-deck pursuits could co-exist. And once the idea of a fixed seating area spread to other vessels, the third of shipboard's serving troika materialised: the cabin and dining saloon steward was joined by the deck steward.

These outdoor men were reassuring stalwarts who served as the seasick passenger's fresh-air conscience. Eyes permanently squinted against mid-ocean glare, their faces, necks and hands were burnished the colour of mahogany, legacy of countless crossings and countless cups of bouillon or tea. They donned sweaters beneath their blue wool uniforms, their jackets impregnated with coal smoke and salt-shiny at the elbow, their Cunard buttons greened by continual Atlantic damp. The deck steward's daylight hours were demanding, combining non-stop activity when the sun shone and chaffing idleness when it did not.

43

Most passengers bound for steamer or deck-chairs have always been a hesitant, equivocal lot. At home, they might remain seated outdoors perfectly content for hours. But their long-term tenancy on deck was affected by too many sea-going variables: the motion might be upsetting, the wind too searching, the glare discommoding, the occupants of an adjacent chair insufferable, the appeal of a passing friend irresistible or, in crueller months, the warmth of the smoking room too inviting.

And after the Second World War, when the Cunard Line undertook the provision of mattress pads and steamer rugs, the deck steward's task of simply installing a passenger in his or her deck chair was formidable. The chair had to be moved into or out of the sun, sheltered from the wind, its mattress spread, the passenger seated, the feet cocooned with a rug and, on chilly days, another draped shawl-like around the shoulders. Every mid-morning, the deck steward dispensed his time-honoured collation of bouillon and later collected each empty cup and saucer. (Shipboard service's inescapable double bind: that which is delivered must also be retrieved.) Passengers seldom vacated their deck chairs for good; that would have been too easy. He or she would doubtless return before the light failed, invariably just in time to enjoy a tea tray in the lap.

But passengers did abandon even the most sheltered promenade decks after dark, a pheno-menon encouraged by the deck stewards. Only at day's end was their ordeal over. Dozens of dis-carded blankets were gathered up, folded and stacked into lockers; chairs were collapsed and lined up into night-storage ranks, leaving decks cleared for the seamen who hosed them down each dawn.

Final word on the walker/sitter controversy from a New Yorker I know who recalls that during crossings as a young bachelor, the promenade deck was a perfect venue for meeting young ladies. He would occupy a deck chair on the circuit and, after spotting a likely candidate passing him unescorted, would immediately begin circling the deck in the opposite direction. Those notorious double en-counters worked to his advantage and before he had logged his first mile, he had struck up an invaluable acquaintanceship that, with luck, would last until Southampton.

If passengers were soldiers and ships a distant cantonment, an evening bugle would signal Retreat; the colours would be lowered, the parade ground deserted, arms stacked and howitzers muzzled as companies withdrew into the casern. The symbolism serves a Cunarder admirably; the sun's colours having been lowered into the sea, the promenade parades were dismissed, walkers and sitters alike surfeited, and a passenger Retreat followed inevitably. Lamplight replaced daylight as interior pleasures beckoned, first to dress, then to dine, then to smoking room, drawing room or library and ultimately to the incomparable pleasure of a good book in a creaking cabin.

Lucania's fireplace: Capacious sofas and over-sized cushions, stained glass, glowing coals, brass scuttle and art-nouveau carpeting around the obligatory sheepskin hearth-rug, offer a snug retreat during North Atlantic winter crossings. (The University Archives, The University of Liverpool)

At night – the beauties of a night on shipboard! – down in your berth, with the sea hissing and fizzing, gurgling and booming, within an inch of your ear; and then the steward comes along at twelve o'clock and puts out your light, and there you are! Jonah in the whale was not darker or more dismal.

Harriet Beecher Stowe, *Night on Shipboard*, 1854

The two great facts of life were food and God.

Ernest Shackleton, about his second polar journey, 1909

What was it that brought passengers lurching so ravenously into the dining saloon each evening? Was it only the prospect of food? Or did they crave something more than yet another variant of salt pork or beef, more than boiled potatoes and cabbage, more than that notorious 'sea pie' with which too many early menus were surfeited, more than a plateful of bruised apples and grapes? One senses that they did, that Cunard was obliged to provide two kinds of transatlantic nourishment: food for the soul as well as the stomach, socio-emotional reward in addition to gustatory satiation. Passengers after dark need companionship and only in the dining saloon, the one public room that could accommodate them all, might those dual pangs be assuaged.

I experienced the same phenomenon crossing on a very different vessel, *Sovereign of the Seas*, the

world's largest cruise ship. My wife Mary and I had embarked for her delivery from St Nazaire where she had been built, to Florida for her entry into Caribbean service. We were two weeks at sea over Christmas 1987 and the New Year, booked for the only line voyage the vessel would ever make.

For that crossing, *Sovereign* offered none of her anticipated passenger perks. There was no need for them; apart from ourselves and several dozen technical people, the ship was empty. We rattled about in a deserted, largely inoperative vessel. Though every public room was furnished, they were devoid of stewards, barmen, entertainers and clients. Vibration added to that haunted atmosphere; late at night, empty bar stools in the deserted Schooner Bar twirled eerily as though just vacated by ghost passengers.

A mood of surreal abandonment suffused both huge vessel and minuscule passenger load. We straggled in to eat thrice daily in one corner of a dining room, helping ourselves from a steam table. Breakfast and lunch were perfunctory, everyone preoccupied with a crushing workload. But after dinner, our stays at table lengthened progressively, trying the patience of stewards anxious to set for breakfast before quitting. Although it was never once articulated, none of us wanted to relinquish that fragile sense of shipboard community. That dining table served as our only social focus and each of us privately despaired of being exiled to vacant lounge, empty corridor and isolated cabin. By prolonging that dining camaraderie, we were duplicating a ritual of crossings past, when ships sailed without dancing, cruise directors, cinemas and cabaret. Thrust abruptly into that simpler transatlantic mode, I readily understood early steamer passengers' fixation with the saloon.

Additional psychological factors may have been at work as well. When I commanded a marine platoon during the Korean War, I noticed that the men's morale seemed markedly lower at dusk each day. A navy surgeon/psychiatrist later suggested that as night fell, spirits sank throughout the division, that officers and men alike needed reassuring cheer. Admittedly, the advent of night in Korea signalled the start of patrolling, reason enough in itself for dread or unease; but something more than combat angst triggered those inevitable evening slumps, an anxiety stubbornly retained from childhood, fear of the dark and the unknown. As in wartime trenches, so on board liners in the midst of a hostile ocean; passengers no less than marines sought solace and passengers found it in the saloon's evening warmth.

At least *Sovereign of the Seas* was stable! The sea motion of early Cunarders was appalling and universal seasickness inevitable. Only during the worst gales today does one glimpse the incessant norm of conditions on board the first steamers. Christopher Morley has immortalised that motion for all time: 'the long slow lift, the hanging pause, the beautiful sinking plunge'. And within the dining saloon the reek of cabbage, the thunder of green water on the deck overhead and the incessant rivulets of sea water staining paint and carpet alike were invariable concomitants of Cunard's early catering.

In the saloon, only three things were not tied down: passengers, stewards and the food. Everything else was either bolted to the deck, suspended

In the days long before bingo, horse-racing or, God forbid, cabaret, Cunard passengers on board the first Caronia pass their evenings in the dining saloon or talking and reading in the library, lounge or writing room.

from the deckhead or locked into racks. Long tables permanently affixed ran fore and aft. Permanent benches flanked each side of the table with backs that, like those on suburban trains, could be reversed after dinner when dining saloon became lounge. Along the walls on either side were permanent padded benches which sometimes doubled as bunks; curtains provided rudimentary walls for this inexpensive saloon accommodation.

Beneath those *ad hoc* berths were lockers for storage of stout crockery, silverware and – ubiquitous early table covering – yards of oil cloth. Its British name, 'American cloth', rewarded Yankee ingenuity for solving that vexing problem of accommodating meals on a table that reproduced every leap and jar of the hull. Indeed, the first glimmering of luxury aboard Cunarders dates from the moment when hulls were stable enough for cabin passengers, at least, to dine off linen rather than American cloth.

But until that moment, sometime in the mid-

1870s, oil cloth was a transatlantic necessity. Consider this early description, earlier than Cunard, of George Pinckard's mid-Atlantic dinner in 1806:

> But scarcely are the things on the table, and the servants stationed, clinging to the backs of our chairs, before a sudden lurch of the ship tumbles all into disorder . . . The soup salutes the lap of one of us; another receives a leg of pork; a third is presented with a piece of mutton or beef; a couple of chickens or ducks fly to another; the pudding jumps nearly to the mouth of the next; and the potatoes are tossed in all directions about the deck of the cabin . . . everything is disorder and confusion.

Note, according to passenger Pinckard, that it was not the plates that left the table, it was the food that left the plates. Every piece of Cunard china was contained within special circular cutouts in a rack or fixed wooden tray. Above the table, a second

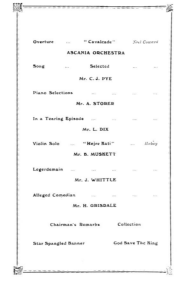

A ship's concert programme that has survived from an Ascania crossing of 1937. Typical of the times, this was the acme of passenger amusement presented from a stage rather than improvised by the passengers themselves. But the performers are all passengers regardless. (Cunard Line)

Changeover on board Tuscania: The start of the entertainment cycle on board Cunarders, a time when the company took a hand in passenger amusement, offering horse racing, cinema and, available only during summer crossings, dancing on deck.

The First Class Smoking Room on board Queen Elizabeth.

Publicity handouts advised passengers that all the panelling was created from one vast tree.

CUNARD LINE

Auld Lang Syne

Farewell Dinner Menu, 2 January 1933, on board the Berengaria. (Cunard)

gimballed rack swayed beneath the lamp, its cut-outs filled with condiments, bottled sauces and stout tumblers.

Subsequently, after linen took over, these racked trays disappeared, replaced by table edges that could be raised. The English called them 'fiddles', the French 'cabarets'. On today's stabilised vessels, even the fiddles are gone. During storms, to prevent things from sliding onto the carpet, stewards wet the tablecloths to increase friction between place setting and linen. Alas, that water has an unpleasant way of seeping down to the edge of the cloth that lies in one's lap so that passengers who have braved the pleasures of a stormy table depart the dining room with inexplicably damp knees.

There is also the testimony of an Englishman called Deane who was booked westbound on board the *Niagara* in 1856. His crossing started off well; the purser moved him to a double cabin and the chief steward seated him at the captain's table. Deane was as flattered as he was surprised though he should not have been; public relations were as important then as now and it was known that Deane was an editor with *The Times* of London.

For the first few days, Deane saw more of his bunk than his coveted table. The little *Niagara* 'struck very bad weather' and he spent an inordinate amount of time 'either lying down before getting up or lying down after getting up'. That wry commentary after the fact is so typical of seasickness, amusing later however grim at the time. That is the nature of the beast, only moments after the infernal motion stops it ceases to be a reality.

Incidentally, one can add an encouraging note about the malady: almost perfect immunity from it is, to my certain knowledge, the sole advantage derived from increasing age. I was once very prone to sea motion but am pleased to report that I survived hurricane Gloria on board *Queen Elizabeth 2* in September 1985 with damp knees as already described but without the need for any medicinal help. Yet the demon still lurks. I felt distinctly unwell onboard a smaller Cunarder, *Sea Goddess I*, in the Caribbean one January. Between Hispaniola and Puerto Rico, Atlantic storm swells rolling through the Mona Passage made us pitch and roll like a cork.

Mealtimes on mid-1850s Cunarders followed closely one after the other. Deane recorded that lunch was at one, dinner at four and supper at ten; breakfast was not mentioned so we must assume it was dispensed at daybreak. Even without any sea motion, it must be wondered that passengers could face dinner only two hours after having concluded lunch. Presumably supper, which Dickens had described as a cold collation on board *Britannia* fourteen years earlier, sustained *Niagara* passengers throughout the night. Deane's spirits improved with the weather. He walked the deck, played whist in the evening and listened to plenty of 'good Yankee stories'. One evening, he thoroughly enjoyed 'an impromptu concert which, liquidated by bowls of punch, lasted 'til long past midnight'.

On board another early Cunarder, the *Tarifa*, an American, John Burgess, was vociferously unhappy with everything. 'All the accommodations for passengers', he began, 'staterooms, dining rooms and toilettes [sic] were in the extreme stern of the vessel at all times.' (*Tarifa* was, in fact, a paddle steamer, so small wonder that everything was aft; better there, Burgess would have discovered, than amidships, cheek by jowl with the

51

machinery and churning paddles.) Service, both cabin and sanitary, was primitive. 'If the steward were wanted, the passengers must go out in the gangway and shout for him. There were only two toilettes on the ship, there was no bath at all', concluded Burgess's melancholy cabin critique.

He was not much happier in the dining saloon, traditional haven for disgruntled clients. It was in the days before swivel chairs so Burgess and his fellow sufferers were crowded along benches. 'At every meal', he lamented, 'there was a free fight for an end seat so that, in case of nausea, one might quickly rush out on deck.' Burgess and his fellow passengers had all been warned. All had received identical printed notices from the chief steward suggesting that 'passengers doubtful of their ability to finish a meal should consider not entering the dining saloon'.

But as Cunard's vessels grew in size, conditions on board improved. Though the reduction in sails was applauded as an advance, it was not lost on passengers that the older sailing steamers were in one sense superior to the new, pure steamers; their press of canvas had helped suppress the most extravagant motion. But the new increased length helped enormously. Just as the longer wheelbase of a car smooths out the bumps, so Cunard's longer hulls evened out the transatlantic ride. These later, less violent crossings were reflected in passenger diarists who dwelt less on adverse conditions, whether sanitary or climatological, than the charms of their fellow passengers.

On a westbound *Scotia* crossing of 1870, a British passenger recalled that each evening they 'gathered in the foresaloon'. This was a subtle territorial expansion – a foresaloon in addition to a main saloon; *Scotia* passengers enjoyed public-room options. There, 'a curiously miscellaneous assembly' dined, including an international benison of bishops – Canadian, Mexican and, always the most numerous, American – bound home from an ecumenical conference in Rome. There was a

temporal leavening as well in the shape of a member of parliament; 'Bismarck Sweeney, Chamberlain of New York (respected by even his political opponents)'; Civil War veterans and large numbers of American expatriates fleeing the Franco-Prussian War.

Conviviality reigned, Cunard's embryonic English-Speaking Union already established. The Britisher confessed that 'I learned more about the various regions of America in a week than long reading could have conveyed'. The message for historians is clear: by 1870, Cunard passengers, rejoicing in additional space, improved conditions and an easier passage, were less preoccupied with discomfort than the vagaries of their fellow passengers. Creature comforts were taken for granted. There were a few tubs in the bathrooms, a smoking room for the gentlemen and a piano chained to the wall of the ladies' drawing room. Individual swivel chairs had been introduced in the dining saloon so rather than an exchange of blows over the end seat,

dinner prompted a congenial exchange of ideas.

The unnamed *Scotia* diarist concluded wistfully:

The days passed all too quickly. I saw with regret that last of the glorious sunsets in the west towards which we were steering and looked back with pleasant memory on the truly social and republican club that broke up in New York Harbour, never all to meet again.

In a previous chapter, it was suggested that boredom almost never clouded Cunard crossings. The only exception arose when the saloon's informal after-dinner routine became codified around the turn of the century for one night only. That celebratory evening, usually near crossing's end, turned into a ponderous crossing fixture known as the ship's concert. It had started innocently enough with a passenger penchant for self amusement. Victorians on both sides of the Atlantic lightened their evenings with parlour readings, songs and

Down in Tourist Class, an intense foursome embarks on yet another rubber of bridge.

Alternative dining on the Queens: For a modest sum, First Class passengers on either Queen Mary *or* Queen Elizabeth *could dine at an extra-tariff restaurant looking high over the stern. This is the* Queen Mary's *Veranda Grill, restaurant by day, night-club by night. The after mast plunges through the band stand.* (Cunard Line)

recitations so it is not surprising that these domestic histrionics should be transferred to Victorian vessels as well.

For years, evening amusement in the saloon remained informal. But someone on *Campania* or *Lucania* – purser or passenger, we cannot be sure – formalised those informal entertainments in the mid-nineties. 'Formal' was the operative word, for evening dresses and boiled shirts were packed into steamer trunks by then and a novel transatlantic elegance reigned. The concert was further legitimised by taking up a collection in aid of seamen's charities. But though the cause was noble, the show was dismal and, within two decades, the institution had already begun to pall. By 1924, Julian Street suggested in his acerbic *Ship-Bored*: 'If you ever decide to end it all, there is one humane suggestion I would make. End it all before the ship's concert.'

Then as now, when in today's cruise idiom the ship's concert is called Passenger Talent Night, there tended to be more passengers than talent. But in every Cunard ship-load there were cabin-loads of sopranos, tenors, baritones, dancers, monologuists, magicians, whistlers, comics, mimics, jugglers and instrumentalists for whom a saloon-load of fellow passengers could be mustered to applaud. In October 1864, a passenger journal had recorded excitedly: 'This evening we are to have an exhibition of prestidigitation', one of the concert's earliest manifestations. Had that pioneer transatlantic magician known what an all-consuming monster he was about to unleash, he might well have left his silks and coins in the stateroom.

In addition to providing an evening's uneven entertainment, the ship's concert gratified a consuming passenger predilection for appointing a committee, a mania that would run rampant during

Franconia's world cruises. The most distinguished passenger on board would be dragooned as its chairman. He – seldom she in those days – was always called upon for some introductory remarks before the hat was passed. Attractive lady passengers were recruited to pass among the audience with ribboned baskets.

The amounts those chairmen could raise varied. In 1911, on board *Lusitania*'s outward crossing of 7 January, £37 11s was collected; on the return, a modest £30 16s 6d was added, for a voyage total of £68 7s 6d. As always, the funds were divided three ways: most went to Britain's Seamen's Orphanage, less to Britain's Home for Aged Mariners and the remainder to what were described only as 'American charities'. A month later, £145 was realised on one *Lusitania* round trip, but her rival *Mauretania* broke Cunard's record in March the same year with a staggering voyage accumulation of £210 14s 10d. Why the disparity, one wonders. Was the *Lusitania*'s mid-winter crossing so rough that only a few passengers braved the concert or did a more persuasive chairman sail in March?

A random sampling of names of Cunard concert chairmen reads like a transatlantic *Who's Who*: Andrew Carnegie, Lord Birkenhead, Andrew Mellon, Ramsay MacDonald the Prime Minister, any number of actors from Tom Mix to John Barrymore, and even young Prince Albert (the future George VI). Just before Christmas 1928 his father the King lay dangerously ill and the prince was hastening home from Royal Naval duties in the West Indies on the *Berengaria*. His birthday fell at sea on 20 December and His Royal Highness took great pleasure in combining it with the ship's concert, auctioning off slices of an elaborate cake that the ship's confectioners had produced for him.

A fancy dress dinner menu from the RMS Berengaria – *30 December 1932.*

Once the slices were gone, he sold the crumbs and over £2,000 was raised for his older brother's, the Prince of Wales's, relief fund for distressed Welsh miners.

In the twenties, there was some relief. *Bona fide* musical performers boarded from the States – jazz bands from American colleges. The Princeton Triangle Club Jazz Band led the parade in 1923, booked both ways on the *Tuscania* with a tour of the continent in between. Other American groups followed suit, enticed by the prospect of an inexpensive summer abroad, playing for passengers en route and then booked solidly at casinos on the continent. Released from final exams in June, student groups were snapped up eagerly by every company's North American management, Cunard's among them.

Since the players were unpaid save for their fare, their presence on board did not violate the Atlantic Conference's strict ban on professional cabaret. Better still, the music they played so enthusiastically was unique on the Atlantic, especially appealing to dimpled, irrepressible eastbound flappers. Cunard evenings during the twenties featured the persistent thump of American syncopation, lyrics sobbed through collegiate megaphones, bobbing brilliantined undergraduate heads, white flannels and blazers, ingenuous grins and the hottest music from New York shows and night clubs.

The new sound overwhelmed Cunard's genteel string orchestras that still played among the palms for afternoon tea. In 1925, the Colgate Collegians as well as the same college's Theta Pi Pipers tootled their way across on Cunard vessels and, in 1927, the Columbia Midnight Sons from New York's Columbia University sailed eastbound on the august *Berengaria* and played their way home at the

55

end of the summer on board *Lancastria*.

By the late thirties, the ship's concert had passed into gentle oblivion, its only vestigial remnant an optional Amateur Night. Hired entertainers supplemented (though never supplanted) those stage-struck passenger/performers who, until then, had monopolised Cunard's evenings at sea. In one sense, the embarkation of professional cabaret – singers, dancers, jugglers, magicians and comedians – achieved a kind of slick professionalism on the North Atlantic although the same boredom as was engendered by amateur concerts has never quite been dispelled by the professionals. Between Caribbean lines especially, a relentless entertainment struggle pits every line against its rival; sadly, it is a war that can be waged but never won. Cunard has sensibly stayed with cabaret, eschewing those interminable production shows, during which, one sometimes longs for the ship's concert.

In 1867, three years before his death, Charles Dickens sailed home to England onboard Cunard's *Russia*. His embarkation mood was in marked contrast to that of his celebrated westbound crossing on *Britannia* in 1842. Then he was new to steamers and had poked fun at the company, but he, as well as Cunard ships, had matured over the intervening quarter century and he wrote about his last Cunard crossing to the company's Chief of Public Relations. He begins with a piece of gratuitous flattery. 'Of all the good ships afloat, mine was the good steamship *Russia*, Captain Cook, Cunard Line, bound for Liverpool. What more could I wish?' So many flowers overflowed 'the small officer's cabin on deck which I tenanted' that additional blooms decorated the dining saloon's empty tables.

At that period of his life, Dickens was an insomniac and we find him wide awake on deck late at night as *Russia* nears her Irish landfall. His keen novelist's eye takes note of 'the vigilant Captain on the bridge, vigilant First Officer looking over the port side, vigilant Second Officer standing by the quartermaster at the compass, vigilant Third Officer posted at the stern rail with a lantern'. Save for the rushing hiss of the benevolent waves and thrum of wind in the rigging, there is no sound save 'an order issued sharply now and then and echoed back'.

Everyone on deck waits, eyes straining forward through the black. Then, 'at the blank hour of two in the morning', the spell is broken: A pinpoint of light flashes far over the bows. The third officer fires two rockets, special signals that will identify *Russia* to those waiting. (Cunard company signals: 'Blue Light, and two Roman candles each throwing six blue stars in quick succession'.) Glittering blue cascades flare above, illuminating *Russia*'s deck-scape. There is no response ashore. Captain Cook's voice comes clearly aft: 'Give them two more rockets, Mr Vigilant.'

The third officer touches a glowing rope-end to additional fuses. Sparks rush aloft and more blue lights tumble through the night. Six pairs of eyes peer into the darkness at the reluctant shore station until 'a little toy rocket is flashed up from it'. Cunarder *Russia* is finally acknowledged and Dickens marvels that, before the light of that responding signal has died away, 'we are telegraphed to Queenstown, Liverpool and London and back again under the ocean to America'.

That reassuring ritual concluded every crossing. Dickens's vigil on deck allows us to share a final Cunard evening at sea, the worknight maritime routine that brought company vessels home safely.

QUEEN MARY

Cigarette companies and cereal box premiums had a field day with Queen Mary *when she first appeared. Her likeness was spread throughout Britain.*

The one-funnelled Queen Mary, *at the start of her career at John Brown's Yard on the Clyde.* (William Morris)

An artist's representation of the giant new Cunarder's trio of funnels, used here as a menu cover on board Queen Elizabeth 2.

(*Below*) *A Queen Mary portrait, artist unknown, showing the ship inbound at Southampton.* (Peter Radmore Collection)

(Below) *Another cigarette card.*

(*Right*) *Stephen Card's portrait of* Queen Mary *under weigh.*

WILL'S CIGARETTES

Q.S.T.S. "QUEEN MARY"

Their hardest day: Stewards
loathe, with reason, the
beginning and end of each
crossing for it involves an
incredible struggle with passenger
baggage.

A STEWARD'S LIFE

I must go down to the seas again,
    where the billows romp and reel,
So all I ask is a large ship that rides
    on an even keel,
And a mild breeze and a broad deck
    with a slight list to leeward,
And a clean chair in a snug nook and
    a nice, kind steward.

Arthur Guiterman, 'Sea Chill', 1933

If this were a screenplay, now would be the moment for a close-up. Our inquisitive camera would forsake pier and landing stage, relinquish aerial footage of new Cunarders persevering across the Atlantic, abandon approach shots of deck, cabin and saloon and, instead, zoom in to show a crewman's face, in this instance the face of a steward.

Why steward instead of passenger, officer, seaman or cruise staff? First, because stewards and stewardesses outnumber every other department on board; second, because their unremitting toil sustains shipboard's most enviable commodity, service; third, because a steward and his passenger share a unique seagoing relationship; fourth, because their presence distinguishes a passenger vessel from a freighter or tanker; and fifth, because they are the most memorable men and women on board. Passengers always remember their stewards – hovering presences whose ministrations have enriched every crossing or cruise since *Britannia*.

Save for that unique solo post, the captain's tiger or personal steward, there are four kinds of steward on board: cabin, deck, bar and dining room. Between them, they sustain shipboard's legendary comforts from the moment passengers first awake until they retire at night; from cabin to deck to lounge to dining room, stewards dispense their special care. In contrast to service ashore, which tends increasingly to indifference, Cunard service afloat has always shone.

Their on-board chores differ. Cunard cabin stewards and stewardesses keep staterooms spotless, beds made, clothes in place on hangers or en route to the laundry and back and, as Leigh-Bennett reminds us, make 'the bath taps twinkle and glazing gleam'. Out in the fresh air, deck stewards are shipboard's weather oracles, purveyors of chair, rug and tray, full of invaluable advice about sun, wind, fog and seasickness. In bars and lounges, accommodating stewards, descendants of those hallowed originals in vanished smoking rooms, appear mystifyingly at our elbow, ready on the instant to fetch us a drink, a smoke or, long before cruise staff, a winning number in the ship's pool. The dining-room steward seats us at least twice daily at an inviting table, whose linen, cutlery, crystal and china he has arranged impeccably. Menu proffered, he attends our every gastronomic whim, however exotic, offering sober recommendation but never reproof.

Yet however congenial and benevolent that steward image, his is a pressured and never-ending job, hard on the nerves, harder on the feet. Stewards are on duty every moment that passengers are on board. And in these times of instant turnaround – in at dawn, out at dusk – today's Cunarders are almost never empty: as one passenger-load disembarks, another takes its place. There are few hours off in port, never any weekends and no days at home for six months at a stretch. Only during a vessel's annual dry docking is the steward ostensibly at ease but his rest, if any,

is tempered with the prospect that, once shipfitters have coiled up their hoses and cables and tracked their last footprints over the carpet, backbreaking hours will be required to restore cabin, corridor, deck, lounge and dining room to passenger readiness.

Cruising has disrupted Cunard stewards' home life. In the old crossing days, when company tonnage was confined almost exclusively to the North Atlantic, turnarounds were positively leisurely. *Campania*, for instance, used to spend a week in Liverpool between sailings, allowing stewards several days at home between voyages to New York and back. Even during the Queens' weekly express service, there was time for two nights' leave at home in Southampton every fortnight. But these days, worldwide cruising schedules, as well as the emphasis on ruthlessly fast turnarounds, mean that stewards are away at sea for months at a time, often strangers to their young children.

But the lure of the ships, no less than the lure of the sea and the lure of the money, remains potent. Regardless of long hours and long absences, the pay, buttressed by tips, was good, often better than the master's. Commodore Sir Edgar Britten used to disembark from *Queen Mary* in Southampton carrying a bundle of dirty shirts under his arm. Each time, he passed a line of expensive motor cars driven by senior stewards' wives waiting to pick up their husbands. Sir Edgar would walk off the pier with his laundry and queue up for a tram.

Moreover, a steward's life at sea was a proud tradition in the port cities of Liverpool and Southampton. Cyril Wareham, who rose through Cunard White Star steward ranks to become restaurant manager of the *Queen Mary*'s Veranda

Grill, was originally a '*Titanic* orphan', one of five children whose mother had been widowed by the loss of her husband, Robert, cabin steward on the ill-fated White Star vessel. Despite his mother's tearful protestations, Cyril had run away to sea as soon as he finished school. As his father before him, he embraced that bittersweet life of travel, separation and, most rewarding, the irreplaceable camaraderie that only shipmates of long standing share.

Stewards have always relished the glamour of their ships, especially a new one. Just as passengers were anxious to sail on the company's largest and fastest, so stewards were pleased to be assigned to them, a mark of prestige and often a prelude to promotion. Just after World War II, when bleak austerity ruled Britain, there were splendid perks on the North Atlantic run. Stewards regularly smuggled home from New York a bi-weekly cornucopia of rationed or unobtainable Yankee delights including nylon stockings, coveted postwar rarities which they distributed lavishly to families and friends all over Southampton.

Stewards are still, in a very real sense, the masters of the ship, maritime factotums who see, hear and discuss all that happens on board. They not only know everything about their jobs, about the company and about other ships in the fleet but about every passenger as well. News of any kind, some verifiable, other wildly inaccurate, travels like lightning on board an ocean liner. A steward on the old *Queen Elizabeth* once suggested that if you exchanged a confidence on the bow and ran to the stern, that same secret, only slightly embellished, would be whispered to you on arrival.

Manning every vessel's intelligence network or bush telegraph was its corps of gregarious, sometimes calumnious stewards. Gossip raced along cabin corridors, interspersed with the whine of vacuum cleaners, to be imparted and chewed over in dozens of cabin pantries or muttered in passing on every staircase. Weightier items were shared along the fo'c'sle head's railing, traditional off-duty vantage point for loquacious stewards, gathered each noon for a smoke before lunchtime's crush. Additional titbits would be exchanged down in the sanctity of the glory hole, the stewards' quarters, as they gathered for a change of jacket or a few precious minutes off. Other news would be passed on late at night in the deafening, jocular fug of the crew bar. The entire ship was the stewards' bailiwick, whether public room and carpeted passenger corridor or through passdoors marked CREW ONLY into the echoing, steel honeycomb of their world.

The following is the story of one Cunard steward. The name tag on his uniform said Eric Stacey for, on board *QE2*, Cunard espoused a new

Eric Stacey poses with Guy and Emily Maxtone-Graham. (Lorayne Killingley)

Genesis of a steward: Young Eric Stacey as an Aircraftsman in Kenya. One wonders whether Lady Dini was the photographer. (Lorayne Killingley)

Stacey, the capable horseman. (Lorayne Killingley)

democratic informality. In the old days, passengers would have called him by his last name only or, preferably, Mr Stacey.

My four children and I boarded *QE2* for the first time in late June 1970. The third, radically different Queen had been in service for just over a year. Formerly, we had crossed regularly on her predecessor *Queen Elizabeth* which, by then, was languishing, neglected and abused, at her Fort Lauderdale berth, a flawed maritime exhibit for incurious Floridians. In those early *QE2* years, the Princess Grill was simply an extra-tariff restaurant, the equivalent of the Veranda Grills on both older Queens; first-class passengers who wished could book a table in the Princess for a mid-ocean night out. There was no Queen's Grill as yet so the Columbia Restaurant served as the vessel's choicest dining room.

It was a handsome, muted space, a Cunard novelty with its low ceiling offset by a position high in the vessel, flanked by rows of windows rather than portholes. (The ship was enveloped in fog for the entire crossing so we saw not a shred of sea or sky for five days, nothing save an opaque white.) At a table near the bottom of the entry steps, we met our stewards – Eric and his younger assistant or commis waiter, Paul Mason, who still serves in the Queen's Grill. It is interesting that at the same time that we passengers meet 'our' stewards, the stewards, in turn, meet 'their' passengers, a two-way dependency unique to shipboard. When assigned a waiter in a restaurant ashore, one seldom becomes 'his' customer in the same sense. That symbiosis is the very lifeblood of the passenger/steward relationship.

Although obviously a senior man, Eric seemed somehow ageless; in fact, he had just turned fifty.

His well-groomed auburn hair was turning silver and he had an olive complexion. His glasses perched on a nose that had apparently been broken at one time. Although he was well under 6ft (1.8m) tall, his slimness gave the impression of additional height. He was extremely soft-spoken and would listen gravely and carefully to every suggestion, clenching his jaw in a distinctive though not forbidding way before responding. He was blessed with an engaging laugh, a kind of sliding chortle that lit up his face. Though he had a keen sense of humour, for the most part Eric was preoccupied with his work, obviously determined to deliver the best.

Yet, devoted as he was to his job, Eric was obviously devoted to children as well. He spoiled mine shamelessly with unceasing, indulgent care. After every lunch and dinner he insisted on picking up the two youngest ones – both quite capable of walking – and carrying them, one on each arm, jubilantly from dining room to cabin.

Many more *QE2* voyages followed, Eric Stacey's dining-room greeting a welcome sequel to embarkation. In 1973, he was promoted to head waiter. Nevertheless, we were always seated in his section of the dining room where he could keep a proprietary eye on Paul Mason, who had succeeded him. By the 1980s, Eric was promoted again, this time as one of the restaurant managers in charge of Britannia (later Tables of the World, now Mauretania) Restaurant. Subsequently, he ran the Princess Grill, by then no longer an optional restaurant but a regular ship's dining room. Eric reigned supreme, resplendent yet never too solemn in black jacket and striped trousers.

Eric Stacey left *Queen Elizabeth 2*, and Cunard, abruptly in January 1984, flying home from Florida

Three faces of Eric, taken from his three Seaman's Discharge books. (Top left) Fresh out of the RAF, he joins Cunard. Next, at the time of the Mauretania strike. (Left) Finally, fifteen years later, Eric Stacey ready to board Queen Elizabeth 2. (Lorayne Killingley)

in the midst of a contract. *QE2* would complete her world cruise without him that year. He was suffering from acute emphysema and I recalled frequent sights of Eric snatching a quick, on-duty smoke in the corridor outside the Princess. Obviously, his lungs were suffering from a lifelong addiction to tobacco. We stayed in touch, by mail from New York or by telephone when I passed through Southampton en route to *QE2*. Although he put up a brave front, it was clear that retirement, such as it was, proved bleak; he missed Cunard's shipboard camaraderie as well as the rhythm and routine of his life at sea. He and his wife had separated some years earlier so that his enforced idleness was passed in solitary quiet, relieved only by occasional visits from his grown-up daughter and grandchildren. The last time we spoke, I invited him to lunch but he made excuses, saying that he no longer went out because a crippling shortage of breath made it impossible. Then, in spring 1988, I had a letter from his daughter, Lorayne Killingley, telling me that her father had died. I was saddened but not surprised; there had been a doomed quality in Eric's voice near the end and I sensed that not only his health troubled him but that life as an invalid held little reward.

That summer, on board *Queen Elizabeth 2*, news of Eric's death preoccupied his dining-room colleagues. In Southampton, I met Lorayne, an attractive, slim woman, with much of her father's looks, married to a detective inspector and the mother of two teenage sons. She talked at great length about her father; though Eric Stacey's shipboard persona was familiar, details of his youth and home life were blank. Only with the help of Lorayne and other members of the family could a predictable yet atypical Cunard career be pieced together.

Eric Stacey was born on 14 March 1920, the fifth of ten children of a Thames harbour dockmaster. He grew up in a crowded, depression-bound Stepney household and, in 1939, like most young Britons, enlisted for the duration. He chose the Royal Air Force and for most of the war served in bombers as a tail gunner, his squadron stationed in Nairobi. That wartime posting initiated a lifelong love of Kenya. During leaves, he struck up a close friendship with a titled woman, and it was presumably through her that Aircraftman Stacey became an accomplished horseman; among the souvenirs he brought home to Stepney from those Kenya years was an inscribed riding crop from 'Lady Dini'.

After demobilisation in England, Eric had to decide on a career. Years earlier, in his late teens,

he had once considered the priesthood, but a taste of theological study led him to abandon the idea. He dreamed of emigrating back to Kenya as a planter but lacked money for the passage out, let alone the price of some land. Finally, through his father's influence, he was admitted to the Merchant Navy Reserve Pool and, in November 1946, Eric Stacey sailed aboard *Highland Chieftain* as an assistant steward. Three months later he went to work for Cunard as a tourist-class waiter on the *Queen Mary*, employment that would continue intermittently until his retirement nearly four decades later.

All British seamen are obliged to maintain a small blue volume known as a Seamen's Record Book and Certificate of Discharge. Its pages serve as a comprehensive record of ships, dates, masters and performance. The early pages of Eric Stacey's first discharge book (there would be three altogether) were all stamped with postwar Cunarders, *Queen Mary, Queen Elizabeth, Caronia* and *Mauretania*. Though his ships changed, his allegiance to Cunard never did, save once.

Opposite a *Mauretania* voyage dated 13 May 1955, the rating column, customarily stamped VERY GOOD, bore instead the ominous legend VOYAGE NOT COMPLETED. Eric Stacey did not sail to New York on *Mauretania* that spring nor for many to follow. He had apparently led a steward's strike, details of which are still not clear; no record of the affair exists in the company's archives, only that *Mauretania*'s departure that month was 'delayed for two days'. According to his family, Eric was championing not his own rights but the rights of some junior colleagues whose living conditions, bunked ten to a cabin, he felt strongly the company should improve.

Although Eric had never been insubordinate, let

alone a trouble-maker, a visual clue hints at the possibility. The identity photograph from his second discharge book, taken in 1952 three years before that strike, betrays a muscular, almost cocky, truculence. He had been a fly-weight boxer in the RAF and one could imagine 32-year-old, pugnacious Eric Stacey dedicated to what he perceived as an injustice to his shipmates and hence participant in that abortive, pierside struggle. Certainly the photograph portrays a different man from the one I knew. By the 1970s he was fully mature, conservative to the point of caution, calm and controlled, almost too calm and controlled; but then Eric of *QE2* was sixteen years older than Eric on board *Mauretania*.

He left Cunard and took a series of jobs ashore. He worked as a waiter at the Polygon, the famous Southampton hotel where his daughter dined with me the summer after his death. He also tried starting a catering business. But in 1959 he went back to sea, working on a series of Shell oil tankers as chief steward. In between ships, he signed up for a month-long course at the London School of Nautical Cookery.

One of the chief steward's duties on board those tankers was that of ship's 'doctor'; Eric Stacey had to become a paramedic and Lorayne remembers that her father practised giving injections on an orange. Once, off Port Said, he needed his own services after injuring his hand badly in an electric fan. After rudimentary treatment in a Saudi Arabian hospital, he had to return to England for extensive surgery and physiotherapy.

Eric went ashore again in 1963 – 'swallowing the anchor' is the sailor's idiom – trying out other Southampton jobs: another bout of catering, a post with a wine merchant and, for three years, work as a car salesman. But the sea still beckoned and miraculously, in 1969, he was rehired by the company, his *Mauretania* ruckus apparently forgotten. The *Mary* and *Elizabeth* were gone and a new Queen had entered service. His fifteen-year Cunard exile at an end, Eric Stacey signed on again. Throughout his remaining days at sea, the employment column of his discharge book was stamped, unvaryingly, *Queen Elizabeth 2*. He had to start at the bottom again, his first post on the new ship simply 'waiter'. But he was exhilarated to be back and, within a year, had been restored to *chef de rang* – full dining-room steward in the Columbia Restaurant.

Near the end: In the early eighties, Eric preparing a special order for one of his passengers. (Lorayne Killingley)

Eric Stacey had married 19-year-old Myra Irving in 1948. Their only child, Lorayne, was born in 1949. Like every seaman's, Eric's days at home were interspersed with regular absences at sea; and like every seaman's wife, Myra was head of the household most of the time but not when her steward/husband came home. Inevitably, domestic friction ensued. A word that every member of Eric's family used in describing him was 'fastidious'. That same fastidiousness doubtless made him an outstanding steward, a job that demands scrupulous order and neatness. But at home in Southampton, relentless fastidiousness provoked repeated quarrels. Lorayne's childhood and adolescence were punctuated by her father's reappearances on leave accompanied by storms of short temper and inevitable parental rows. She recalls him as a heavy smoker, but a smoker who forbade cigarettes in his MG sports car which was kept pristine in the garage. He also complained loudly about ash on the carpet and was upset when Lorayne wore jeans in the high street.

Finally, on coming home one leave in 1975, Eric found his home empty; Myra had left him. On board *QE2*, he said that the break-up of his marriage had come as a complete surprise. To those not privy to the years of preceding strife, it seemed incomprehensible. But the amiable shipboard Eric Stacey apparently bore no resemblance to the uncompromising martinet of 32c Bassett Wood Drive. On board, one heard only about the roses in the garden or the glittering car in the garage,

Eric Stacey ashore somewhere in the Far East. He remained fastidious and impeccably dressed to the end of his life. (Lorayne Killingley)

nothing of the unceasing domestic wars that had destroyed his marriage. For the last thirteen years of his life, he would return on leave to a household that remained his alone.

Worse, after illness forced him to sign off with Cunard, he enjoyed almost no companionship. His focus and friends were at sea on board *QE2*; there was precious little company at home. As he weakened, the estranged Myra shopped and cared for him when she could; but she did not come back to live. In spring 1988, he had to go into the hospital. Lorayne drove down several times from Amersham to see him. She remembers her last visit clearly. Her father had been washed and dressed for her arrival but the collar of his hospital pyjamas was badly pressed. 'He would have been so upset', she said afterwards. As it was, he spent much of that last meeting between father and daughter smoothing and straightening his turned-over top sheet, Eric Stacey's relentless fastidiousness dogging him to the end.

He died on Saturday 30 April 1988 at the age of sixty-eight. His body was cremated and, that August, Lorayne and her mother scattered his ashes at sea from a Solent ferry. Lorayne wrote: 'The officer arranged for the boat to be slowed down for us and as I scattered the ashes and flowers, he took off his hat and saluted, which seemed to add something special to the occasion.'

Nothing could have been more fitting than that Eric Stacey should have returned once again to the sea, into those same coastal waters through which he had sailed so many times on Cunarders. Save for his long banishment, his was a career typical of many Cunard crewmen. One wonders what might have happened in 1946 had demobilised Eric Stacey returned to Kenya, or after 1955 had he not taken part in the strike.

But lives, like ships, follow their own course relentlessly, and hundreds of Cunard passengers must have enjoyed sharing a fraction of Eric's onboard *QE2*. Among his papers and photographs was a *QE2* envelope in which I had once enclosed a tip. On the outside was written: 'Eric: The end of a splendid crossing and one that would not have been the same without your attentive, devoted and very special brand of service.' He had kept that envelope all those years; perhaps it should serve as epitaph for that much-admired and dedicated Cunard steward.

SOUTHAMPTON TERMINAL

THE CUNARDER

- Chris Woods -

QUEEN ELIZABETH

At the Ocean Terminal in Southampton: Eastbound passengers have boarded the boat train for Waterloo as it pulls away from the terminal and their vessel. From a painting by Chris Woods.

Stephen Card's painting of Queen Elizabeth *steaming out of New York harbour, followed in the distance by* Britannic. (Stephen Card)

A Moran tug noses against Queen Elizabeth's port bow plating in New York. (Louis O. Gorman)

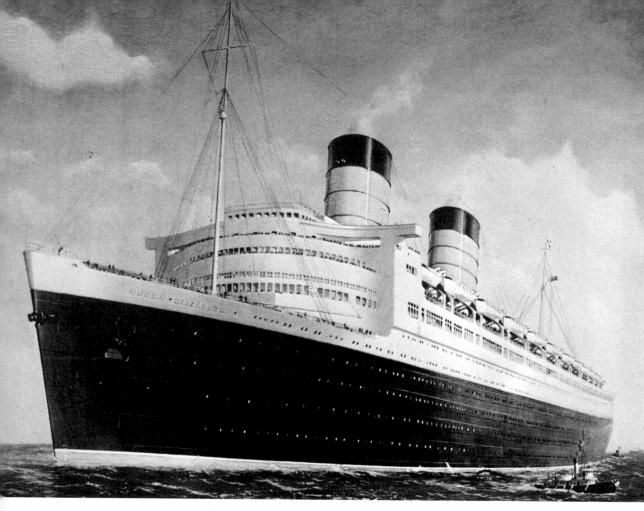

Dream and reality: Two studies, one a painting, the other a photograph. In the painting, note how the unknown artist has minimised the tug's size to emphasise the Elizabeth's bulk. The photograph shows the vessel herself assisted by a trio of tugs as she approaches her Southampton berth. (Cunard Line)

Cigarette cards again: The Ogden Cigarette Company publicise the second Queen with their pre-war packs. If the artist had returned three decades later, he would have added an outdoor swimming pool to the view of the after decks.

OGDEN'S CIGARETTES

THE "QUEEN ELIZABETH"

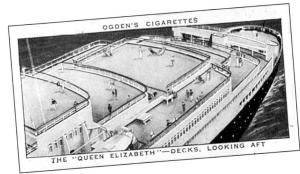

OGDEN'S CIGARETTES

THE "QUEEN ELIZABETH"—DECKS, LOOKING AFT

OGDEN'S CIGARETTES

THE "QUEEN ELIZABETH"—TOP DECK

After transformation into the Seawise University, the fabled Queen Elizabeth burned and sank at her Hong Kong anchorage in 1972.

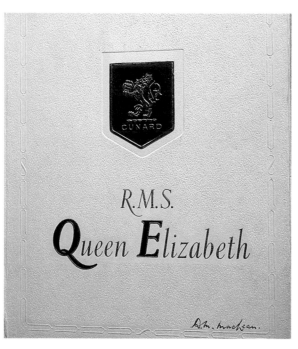

John Young's portrait of the second Queen entitled 'Mid Atlantic 1938'. (John Young)

Queen Elizabeth tied up at Fort Lauderdale in 1968, neglected and abused. (Joseph Schmitz)

Mauretania, *during her North Atlantic days.*

FRANCONIA'S WORLD CRUISE, 1937

In these days of wars and rumors of wars, haven't you ever dreamed of a place where there was peace and security, where living was not a struggle but a lasting delight? Of course you have. So has every man since the beginning of time.

Prologue title card to the film of
Lost Horizon

As the *Franconia* nosed her way down the broad waters of the Hudson, I felt as happy as any of the eager, laughing holiday throng who crowded the decks . . . My chart room was literally piled to the roof with charts for we were to visit many strange places never touched before . . . There was no hurry, no Blue Riband of the Atlantic to hold or reclaim; just long, lazy days of enchantment . . . chasing sunshine and happiness.

Commodore Sir Edgar Britten,
recalling his 1929 world cruise

Always awaited was the appearance of the whites, that symbolic maritime moment when officers and crew changed from North Atlantic blue into tropical white. Masters had, and still have, sole prerogative in choosing that day, one of their few decisions not detailed in company regulations. Governed neither by date, latitude nor itinerary, whites were donned when the captain felt it was time.

And for their passengers, the first whites marked the crossing of a long-anticipated Rubicon, emergence from northern cold into southern warmth. The chill of New York harbour forgotten, wool

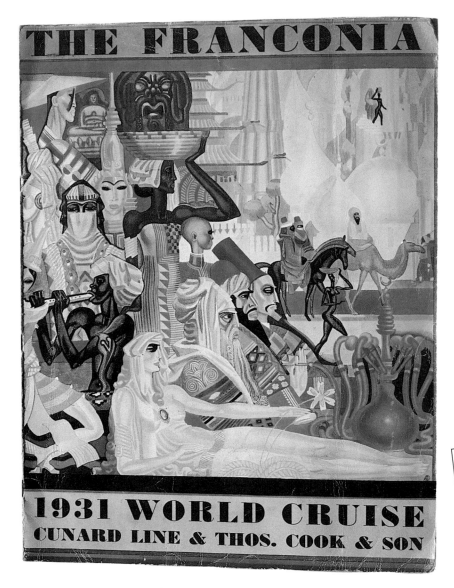

THE FRANCONIA

1931 WORLD CRUISE
CUNARD LINE & THOS. COOK & SON

Artwork from the Franconia's 1931 world cruise. Although the year is different, the mood was not. (Peter Radmore Collection)

Mornflake Oats and Will's Cigarette cards show Franconia, *changing from standard Cunard North Atlantic black to cruising white.*

jackets, fur collars and golf sweaters were consigned to wardrobe trunks, cotton replaced tweed caps and cabin stewards were kept busy loosening heavy brass hexagonal nuts securing stateroom ports. Warmth heralded world cruising.

Franconia was the second Cunarder christened thus. Repeating ship's names became a company practice that arose partly out of the carnage of World War I; abandoning the identity of those torpedoed liners only underscored their loss. So, during the postwar rush of replacement, phoenix-like building, single-funnelled *Franconia, Laconia* and *Ansonia* steamed in place of their two-funnelled predecessors. At the same time, ancient names from the past were recycled as well, *Ascania, Samaria* and *Scythia* among them.

Of all Cunard profiles, perhaps none is more familiarly typical than that single, orange-red, black-topped stack centred atop a boxy 20,000-ton hull. Those intermediates may have lacked the speed, size and splendour of the company's

Mauretania, *when she turned permanently to West Indian cruises. The change in hull colour said it all.*

Their long vigil rewarded, visitors wish bon voyage to Franconia *friends as the vessel sails on her 1937 world cruise at midnight. (Below) Twenty-four hours later, she was headed for the sun.* (The Ocean Liner Museum)

flagships; the express liners *Mauretania, Aquitania* and *Berengaria* still hold centre stage as the great Cunarders of the twenties. But their smaller sisters had special perquisites; they were splendid sea boats, commodious and extremely comfortable. Moreover, they had the exquisite advantage, as significant in naval architecture as in life, of youth.

Those great three- and four-funnelled Edwardian relics were not actually that old. In 1923, the year of the second *Franconia*'s debut, only *Mauretania* was entering middle age; *Aquitania* and *Berengaria* (ex *Imperator*) had been launched roughly ten years earlier. Yet however majestic, they were dated in regard to certain prosaic aspects, lacking adequate bathrooms, a glossy enough second class and overall flexibility. Survivors of a bygone era, they had been launched for a glitter-or-grime traffic that no longer existed. Mass immigration was over and a burgeoning middle class from both sides of the Atlantic demanded affordable as well as comfortable space. All three of those grand old chargers would be turned out to cruise pasture during the depression, but they were awkward cruise ships; too many tourist passengers overflowed first-class

80

space never designed for use by one cruising class. *Mauretania, Aquitania* and *Berengaria* were not only getting old, they were old-fashioned as well.

But those unassuming single-stackers were new as well as newbuilt, invaluable blood stock for Cunard's postwar stable, readily adaptable to fixed or new races. While workhorses *Ascania* and *Samaria* plodded year-round to Canada and back, world-class thoroughbreds like *Laconia* or *Franconia* could leave their New York starting post and canter blithely around the long circumnavigational track each New Year.

How did that replacement *Franconia* differ from the first? What new deck or interior configurations qualified her for cruising better than her predecessor? One answer was capacity. Both *Franconia* hulls were nearly identical, the first 625ft (190.5m) overall, the second 624ft (190.2m); the second boasted an additional 26in (66cm) of beam. Regardless, the earlier *Franconia* could absorb an enormous capacity: 2,850 in all three classes – 300 in first, 350 in second and a dense immigrant crush down in third. She could, in fact, accommodate more than *Queen Elizabeth 2, Sagafjord* and both *Sea Goddesses*

combined, though for those on the lower decks, certainly not in contemporary comfort. Most *Franconia* third-class berths were what was described as temporary, (ie they could be collapsed and stacked in a corner so that cargo might supplant immigrants on eastbound crossings).

The second *Franconia*'s class size reflected postwar priorities. First was smaller – only 240 because of more private bathrooms – while second was larger with 560 rather than 350. Third was the most changed, accommodating less than half the immigrant hordes packed into *Franconia I*. The reason was simple, the end of mass immigration meant the end of berthing compartments. Everyone had a cabin now, however modest. All those lower-deck cabins, as well as most second-class cabins, would be closed off for world cruises. Yet the second-class dining room would be used. Second-class passengers on the new *Franconia* dined in spacious elegance; their saloon had been radically upgraded in order that world-cruise passengers, whether seated in first- or second-class saloons, would enjoy decorative parity.

A glance at the two *Franconia* profiles indicated

other changes. The first one's bridge was separate from the deckhouse, the gap between given over to cargo hold No 4. Those holds were intrusive space-wasters, penetrating six levels down to F- or main deck. Since the second *Franconia* did not need that cargo hold, additional square feet of deck, exterior as well as interior, could be realised. An invaluable boat-deck clear expanse was created behind the bridge as well as additional public rooms on promenade deck just below, extra cabin space below that and a splendid swimming bath down at the bottom. Thus, a 'Pompeiian Bath' and squash court occupied lower-deck space on *Franconia II* that on *Franconia I* had been required as trunk storage for her vast passenger-load.

On promenade deck, a roll-call of public rooms from aft to forward on both ships conveys the emergence of a more spacious first class. On *Franconia I*, there had been an open veranda café overlooking the stern, then a smoking room, gymnasium, lounge and, overlooking the bow, a combined library and writing room. On the second *Franconia*, the space devoted to the veranda café had been incorporated within a larger smoking room, an expansion required by the admission of ladies. The gymnasium, now down below with pool and squash court, was replaced by flanking garden lounges duplicated from larger originals on board *Aquitania*. A writing room and separate card room had no view ahead because that space had been devoted instead to some small but pleasantly situated promenade-deck cabins with prospects to either side or over the bow.

Finally, it was clear that *Franconia* was committed to ambitious cruising. She dressed for the part each autumn, emerging from dry dock sporting a bleached hull – tropical whites of her own – and

green boot-topping that seemed a prescient fore-taste of the second *Caronia*'s startling verdant livery of the late forties. Let us examine *Franconia*'s 1937 world cruise. The year is chosen because better documentation exists and also because that year summons up in retrospect an image of peace, of passenger shipping as usual. It would not be her last; she would circumnavigate the globe over the winters of 1938 and 1939, disembarking her final world-cruise passengers at New York's Pier 54 in early summer 1939, only months before the Nazis marched into Poland. And though the Sino-Japanese conflict already raged in the Far East by 1937, Europe seemed more at peace, Europe before the Anschluss, Europe before Munich, Europe before trenches in Hyde Park.

Franconia steamed into a bitterly cold New York harbour on 2 January 1937, under the command of Captain Dolphin. Only seventy-two first-class passengers had embarked in Liverpool, rattling about in a nearly deserted ship for that winter crossing. Of those Britishers, only thirty would sail on the world cruise. They disembarked and put up at New York hotels while their ship was fuelled, victualled and loaded with mail; *Franconia* would carry the US mails on her odyssey as far south as Rio and Capetown.

Veteran cruise director Ross Skinner and a corps of twelve hardworking assistants trooped on board and began their annual January rite, setting up a cruise office on the port side of the deserted second-class lounge. (One of those keen young assistants was Sheridan Garth who, a decade hence, would be in charge of *Caronia*'s world cruises.) All of them save one Frenchman were American, as would be the majority of their 265 passengers. Throughout the cruise they would cope in a thousand ways, arranging shore excursions, dancing with unattached lady passengers, organising deck sports and bridge tournaments, teaching foreign languages, performing endlessly, whether crossing the equator or topical reviews, and, overall, 'making nice' with the passengers. It was a relief to be on board at last, after weeks ashore at Thomas Cook's Manhattan headquarters obtaining and attaching visas to world-cruise passengers' passports, sent ahead by their owners from home.

In addition to that ample cruise staff, two social directresses, two ministers and a dental surgeon boarded, also a special ship's photographer, among whose darkroom bag of tricks would be printing paper that could double as passenger postcards. Charles Batchelder was the ship's only professional lecturer although there would be passenger amateurs aplenty. He boarded with enough notes and glass slides to deliver sixty-three talks over the ensuing months in the shape of dozens of 'illustrated travelogues' interspersed with doses of current events.

The night of 6 January arrived. *Franconia* lay glittering at Pier 54, her white flanks agleam through the winter night, frosted whiter still near the waterline. Steam crystallised in the bitter air as deck winches fore and aft loaded final stores and trunks, stewards and stevedores alike bundled against the cold. Passengers reached the pier earlier than usual, advised to do so by their first world-cruise bulletin sent through the post: 'In view of the usual excitement and the many details of leave-taking, plan to reach the pier at least two hours in advance of the hour of sailing.' *Franconia* would sail at five past midnight so passengers began arriving at the pier from 8pm onwards.

Foremost among those 'details of leavetaking'

Franconia hits her tropical stride. Passengers had at their disposal the garden lounge, with a seat at the bar or in one of the wicker chairs, or perhaps, the deep shade of the Promenade Deck. (The Ocean Liner Museum)

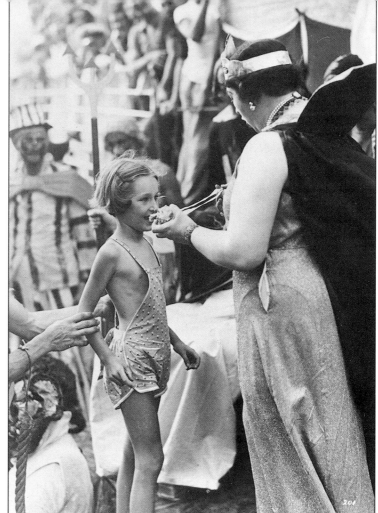

Neptune day celebrations.
Captain Dolphin officiates as
Franconia is greeted into
Neptune's domain. One of the
officers being dumped into the
pool has sensibly worn no socks.
(The Ocean Liner Museum)

were flocks of family and friends who forsook Manhattan's bright midtown lights to descend to the cavernous gloom of Pier 54. Perhaps because of the late hour, they were spared the visitor's customary boarding fee of a contribution to seamen's charity. As those nocturnal figures materialised on the pier, one could instantly distinguish visitor from passenger. Visitors carried nothing but flowers, boxes of books or perhaps an improbable *bon voyage* fruit basket shrouded in amber cellophane. Passengers were encumbered with last-minute purchases, camera bags and jewel cases, that precious luggage never surrendered to porters. As a final distinction, most passengers were lightly clad; their winter overcoats would be redundant in two days and by the time they returned to New York it would be summer. As a result, many clutched raincoats about them against the chill while other brave souls dashed from taxi to gangway in evening dress or black tie, legacy of a festive farewell ashore.

As sailing time approached, raucous late-night greetings and the clatter of high heels on concrete echoed within the pier shed. Oblivious of determined porters crying out at their backs with loaded trolleys, *Franconia* passengers and their friends laughed, hugged and finally swept shivering and chattering across the gangplank. On board, there was more laughter and more chatter, warmed by a champagne nightcap down in the cabins.

Only after a brass-buttoned page had paraded up and down the passageway battering a Chinese gong for the third time and only after *Franconia*'s steam whistle had twice rent the night with a peremptory summons to sea, did visitors tear themselves away. Embarkation lobby farewells were repeated from the pier; determined leavetakers braved the cold to shout and wave across a widening expanse of black river. *Franconia* slipped her hawsers, tugs backed her out into the Hudson and swung her bows downstream. Then, the twinkle of her decklights haloed with frost, she steamed off alone towards the Narrows, paradoxically bound for but detached from the world. Her first call would be Trinidad's Port of Spain.

During some world cruises, *Franconia*, like a reluctant deck walker in winter, did not complete her circuit. In 1927, she had embarked her passengers for a cruise of the Northern and Southern Hemispheres at the end of which circumnavigation had not been achieved at all. The vessel had steamed east from New York to Hong Kong through the Mediterranean and Suez Canal, then returned home around the Cape of Good Hope. The point that year and the following year was to avoid the long Pacific crossing, dismissed as 'a homeward voyage possessing very little of interest in proportion to the vast amount of time and distance involved'.

Yet in years to come, that much-maligned Pacific would be traversed in both directions, offering westbound passengers the bonus of extra hours of sleep as clocks were put back. But in 1937, 1938 and 1939, *Franconia*'s cruise finales would be eastbound crossings, subjecting those passengers to a succession of shorter, 23-hour sea days. Presumably, by then, Cunard White Star planners had learned that clients booked for world cruises could survive and might even relish that long crossing.

But in early January 1937, that Pacific coda lay far over *Franconia*'s bows; passengers were preoccupied with that Atlantic overture, torn between keeping warm on deck and unpacking chores awaiting them below. World-cruise passengers brought more clothes than any other *Franconia*

85

Some of the mannequins for the fashion show pose out on the Boat Deck. (The Ocean Liner Museum)

In contrast to most world cruise passenger-loads, Franconia's was not all old. (The Ocean Liner Museum)

passenger-load. This was no nine-day crossing and continental tour but a half-year's shipboard tenure, and the convenience of embarking and disembarking at the same port encouraged indulgence in the matter of belongings, especially clothing.

During the southeasterly crossing from St Helena to Cape Town, 'A Tropical Fashion Show, Solving the Eternal Question of What to Wear' was held on board. Selected passenger models paraded around the main lounge before a packed house, dressed appropriately for walking through the rain forest at Victoria Falls, kitted out for the Indian overland train or exploring the ruins of Angkor. Significant about those mid-ocean mannequins of half a century ago was that their clothes were not borrowed from on-board boutiques (*Franconia* had none) but belonged to the passengers, all of whom had embarked equipped for every contingency.

Thomas Cook had not been much help. Their only advice had been to pack rain gear and overshoes but to delay purchase of solar topees until landfall in Africa or India where they would be better and cheaper. But other evidence indicates that most male passengers, at least, came prepared for the worst, outfitted for high adventure. Sir Edgar Britten recalled in 1929 that his world-cruise passengers had boarded with 'umbrellas, sunshades, tinted sun spectacles, fans, cameras (still and cine), binoculars, pedometers, altimeters, small clothes-lines and pegs in neat packages from the department store, flasks (thermos and otherwise) and drinking cups'.

But *Franconia*'s baggage glut was not confined to gadgets. If their husbands were equipped for excursions ashore, lady passengers had brought trunkfuls enough for shipboard excursions – those nightly, couturial descents to dinner. Many world-cruise

Shuffleboard tournament, ladies semi-finals. Note the elegance of the deck chair occupants – ties and jackets retained, cloth-caps temporarily removed. (The Ocean Liner Museum)

regulars knew each other from previous voyages and a subtle but competitive edge coloured each lady's wardrobe selection for the dining saloon. But in the matter of table selection, peace reigned. Chief Steward Rigby's chores were made easier on world cruises, again because so many of the old hands were friends; they knew exactly where and with whom they wished to eat, in effect arranging their own contented seating. Despite some inevitable shuffling among the newcomers, both dining saloons settled down nicely.

As soon as stewards wheeled those emptied trunks down to D-deck's baggage room, a deluge of paper began accumulating under cabin doors. That proliferation of cruise ephemera included health tips that long experience had taught ship's physician J. E. Thoresby to circulate at the beginning of every southern voyage. Ladies were asked never to play deck tennis in high heels – sound advice but unnecessary, one would have thought, for an experienced shipboard clientèle. Anticipating the heat to come, Thoresby warned passengers to eat moderately (hopeless precaution on any vessel), to seek shade from the dread tropic sun and not to play their cabin fans directly on themselves while sleeping. His only bizarre advice was the recommendation that shore excursionists soap the inside of their socks 'to avoid friction and blisters'. Thoresby concluded with a hoary south-seas caveat: 'There is no truth in the popular belief that alcohol keeps away malaria and other fevers.'

After Trinidad, *Franconia* deserted the Caribbean and settled down to long sea days en route to Bahia and Rio, dawdling along at a comfortable 15 knots. Cruising suited *Franconia* and a profile designed for fearsome North Atlantic gales adapted well to tropic peace. The white-painted vessel seemed

Joseph Boxhall, one of Franconia's *officers, a survivor from the* Titanic *tragedy twenty-five years earlier.* (The Ocean Liner Museum)

perfectly at home, no longer labouring across a hostile ocean but sliding over sparkling waters, sole occupant of a benign seascape. At successive ports of call, where pilot, stevedore, agent and shopkeeper waited, first glimpse of *Franconia* was a lazy smoke smudge on the horizon, followed by the brilliant glare of a sunstruck bridge screen until, closer inshore, her glistening hull mirrored a restless wash of foam along the waterline.

On board, a soothing indolence descended. As his vessel reeled off a patient 350 miles (650km) each day, Captain Dolphin's log extracts told the tale. Cape Hatteras's 'fresh breeze, moderate sea, cloudy and rainy' had given way to Nassau's 'moderate wind and sea, clear and fine' which in turn gave way to Trinidad's 'light airs and smooth sea, fine and clear'. Those enviable conditions would obtain for the entire 35,000-mile (64,860km) voyage; 'flying fish weather', Captain Dolphin suggested in one of his soothing weekly bulletins issued from the cruise office. Off Bangkok in

88

March, one passenger remarked that he had not seen a wave since Rio de Janeiro, such was the consistent calm of those southern waters.

The rule was, outdoors whenever possible. That ubiquitous tropical glare was tamed into a deck chiaroscuro, bounded by sun-dappled railing, the restful depths of covered promenades and, newly rigged over much of boat deck, blessed canvas awning. White-clad crew and passengers sought shade save forward on B-deck, just under the bridge, where carpenters had erected the ship's outdoor swimming bath, occupants of which enlivened the vista for bored junior officers fulfilling their four-on-eight-off bridge watches above.

Behind the bridge, awnings and wind baffles were rigged to create *Franconia*'s Starlight Theatre, a protected outdoor venue for films, concerts and illustrated lectures. In the twenties, silent films had been screened up there after dinner 'with musical interpretations by the ss *Franconia*'s orchestra', as though passengers were at home in an Odeon. But by 1937, talkies had long since created their own sound so, during film evenings, bandmaster Teddie Westfield and his men enjoyed an evening off.

Luncheon moved outdoors as well. Cool buffets were spread aft along B-deck, inviting aspics, mousses and galantines trembling with the engines' vibration beneath canvas shade strung across second-class promenades. Passengers lunched seated on folding chairs. Quaintly, they were discouraged from table hopping, requested earnestly instead to duplicate their dining-saloon groupings 'to enable stewards to give personal attention to their passengers'.

Below decks, as the warmth increased, wind-scoops were attached to cabin ports and forward corridor doors were left ajar to absorb even the faintest breeze. The vessel filled with excess humidity, accumulating sea-damp that raised havoc with starched table linen, ladies' hair and every ship's piano, not only the encased upright on boat deck but the main lounge's great Bechstein as well.

Although Captain Dolphin began one of his bulletins with 'It's just been sizzling', *Franconia*'s most taxing hot-weather ordeal – a following wind in the infamous cauldron of the Red Sea – luckily did not materialise for 1937's itinerary. Wind over the stern would retain a noisome envelope of stack gasses around the ship for hours. Seeking occasional relief, her master would order the vessel turned through 180 degrees, steaming back to the north on a reciprocal course for a few miles until head winds had ventilated *Franconia*'s 'tween decks sufficiently; then he would resume course to the south.

When not asleep in their cabins, splashing in the canvas pool or lazing in deck chairs, *Franconia* world-cruise passengers set about organising themselves. Just as they had been welcomed on board by Cunard White Star as 'members' of the cruise, so they in turn reinforced that membership mentality by submitting to an extraordinary hierarchy of committees and clubs. Despite the presence of a large cruise staff, passengers retained their traditional, transatlantic autonomy. A two-passenger general committee oversaw a larger executive committee chaired by cruise director Ross Skinner; its membership included his entire staff and was given additional authority by the presence of Staff Captain Pope as vice-chairman.

But that was only the tip of the iceberg. Skinner's executive committee spawned an entertainment committee and a sports committee. Entertainment had four sub-committees – music, dance, bridge

The sight that greeted so many footsore world cruise passengers: the return on board, the most exquisite part of every shore excursion. (The Ocean Liner Museum)

and horse racing, while Sports oversaw shuffle-board, deck tennis, gymkhana and squash. Anyone deprived of a committee membership joined clubs instead, a club for book lovers, a club for music lovers, a club for still cameras or a club for cine cameras.

Franconia's most popular sports fixture from the twenties no longer survived. These were boxing matches between crew departments, fought in a full-size ring erected in the adaptable Starlight Theatre, courtesy of the gymkhana committee. They had proved enormously popular and were always preceded by enthusiastic passenger betting. Regrettably, those three 2-minute rounds between 'T. Cranks (deck) and F. Dandy (baker)' tended not to end with the final bell but recurred later, below decks, long after the ring had been dismantled. Cunard's head office had put a stop to them.

Periodically, those languid sea days were disrupted by approach to land. Pursers changed Brazilian for South African money and additional barrages of schedules and pamphlets were thrust under cabin doors. The evening before, Skinner and his staff held what were called 'travel forums' in the main lounge where Batchelder had set up his projector and screened hand-tinted views of the morrow's exotica. And then, early on the morning of the ship's arrival, the port-side promenade-deck railings would be packed with passengers – still and cine club members to the fore – craning for a view of a municipal welcoming ceremony while awaiting the call to the pier. How many of them, one wonders, had soaped the insides of their socks?

Two attractive shore perquisites graced every *Franconia* landfall. First, rather than clamber into buses to see the sights, passengers were accommodated in touring motors, holding no more than seven each. Unlike the buffets on the after end of B-deck, car groupings changed like the tide between ports; cruise young who had dutifully boarded cars with their parents in Rio deserted them by Cape Town, motoring instead with their peers. And by Yokohama, they and their elders would make it their business not to be seated anywhere with certain fellow passengers, unavoidable ostracisms endemic to long cruises.

The second great port perk was that everywhere passengers were made to feel so welcome. By 1937, *Franconia, Carinthia* and *Laconia* had blazed a firm global trail; Cunard vessels steamed annually into Colombo, Bombay, Singapore and Hong Kong, to mention but four calls of an exotic dozen. Those world-class Cunarders materialised frequently enough to be remembered but infrequently enough not to cloy. Too many present-day Caribbean vessels, locked into relentless weekly itineraries, soon wear out their welcome; local enthusiasm for those visits, however beneficial to the economy, inevitably wanes.

Not so for *Franconia* in the thirties. Ever since they had handled Cunard's first world cruises, Thomas Cook had utilised their far-flung network of assistance, information and, most important for cruising, reception in every port. That kind of global cruise savvy takes years to establish, as the French Line's Raymond-Whitcomb charter to South America would demonstrate the following year, 1938. Then *Normandie* tore south from New York on her first cruise ever, having embarked a thousand passengers anxious for a lavish, pre-Lentern binge in Rio de Janeiro. Only after they had disembarked into the carnival hugger-mugger of Brazil's port capital did they discover that tickets to the most coveted municipal balls were unavailable

91

and should have been booked at least a year before. Luxuriating in first class afloat, *Normandie* passengers were reduced to second-class trippers ashore. The French Line, expert in New York or Le Havre, had proved woefully out of its depth in Rio.

By contrast, Cunard and Thomas Cook's world-cruise continuum oiled the way everywhere. Quite simply, passengers were cherished; every club, hotel, shop and entrepreneur along *Franconia*'s itinerary vied for the privilege of entertaining or extending some special service, less ambush than anxiety to please. South Africa's welcome, for instance, ranged from the predictable to the practical, from a Cape Town beauty shop wooing lady passengers with treatments to 'smooth away the coarseness and dryness caused by the sea voyage' to their husbands' guest membership in the Royal Durban Golf Club.

Batavia's Harmonie Club got up a dance 'for all passengers' who, for that evening alone, were granted honorary membership; music was supplied by Teddie Westfield's vastly superior *Franconia* musicians who brought ashore up-to-date musical arrangements in their music cases. Raffles Hotel in Singapore fêted *Franconia* passengers around the clock, proposing 'tiffin in the Veranda Ballroom' and, later that night, a Grand Cruise Ball 'open to Singapore residents'. And in that twilight of empire, it could be safely assumed that those anonymous 'residents' would be the colony's top drawer. There were no air tourists to dilute the mix, indeed there were few other travellers of consequence in port save the newly landed *Franconians*.

Nothing was quite as provincial as the jaded insularity of far-eastern colonial outposts, so the promise of *Franconia*'s orange-red funnel looming over the waterfront's shabby godowns and cranes was just as exhilarating a signal to the port's establishment as to its merchants. New faces would enliven the evening, new clothes would grace the veranda, new gossip would titillate, new tunes would echo beneath ballroom punka fans. The remote, unattainable West was in town, just as rare and exotic for the colonials as anything east of Suez.

Bård Kolltveit, the Norwegian marine historian, has so rightly compared a cruise ship's docking to the apparition of some wondrous alien being materialising out of a blue infinity, visitation as though from another planet. He stresses that it is a two-sided, reciprocal vision; passengers peer down at locals no less curiously than locals peer up at passengers. And as long as *Franconia* remained in port, as long as her passengers trooped down the gangway to board their motors, as long as they clambered giggling into rickshas, as long as they thronged souk, bazaar, temple, ruin or club, so would the port's inhabitants throng pier and gangway in turn. The mighty boarded to inspect *Franconia*'s interior, the humble crowded mutely beyond the pier gate, staring at that profile floating miraculously above the mundane waterfront.

Franconia's welcome extended all the way around the world. At Colombo, Lavinia Beach hotels offered passengers unlimited bathing privileges along beaches which, cruise director Ross Skinner assured his flock, had been rendered 'shark proof'. It goes without saying that the hoteliers were amply repaid by drink and lunch orders. (Their mood stands, once again, in sharp contrast to the stance of Caribbean hotel managers who, faced with an influx of dread cruise passengers today, seldom extend any privileges. Indeed, during one *QE2*

Christmas cruise long ago, one all-consuming passenger sport was insinuating oneself from public beach into hotel pool.) In China, producers of the traditional shadow plays were ready for the world cruise with a special production entitled THE RMS Franconia IN THE STREETS OF PEIPING.

It is difficult to compare 1937's cruising costs with today's; the value differential is so unreal. Then $5 equalled £1 although the dollar was standard currency on board the American-infested *Franconia*. It had considerable purchasing power half a century ago; $8 for instance took care of all a passenger's tips each week, to cabin to lounge to deck to dining room. (Traditionally, world cruisers tipped every Sunday.) Deck chairs were free for the entire voyage, and rugs and cushions cost only $2.50 for five months' use. A single dollar paid a full year's membership in Cunard White Star's Cruising Club and if passengers brought drink in bulk from ashore, the chief steward's cooperage was only $1 a case. Back home on the pier, US passengers would be permitted $100 of duty-free purchases.

But paradoxically, those strong dollars were vulnerable. Halfway through the cruise, they started running out. Monies circulated as tips within the ship's economy remained on board; but a serious currency drain arose from the passenger habit, encouraged by the cruise staff, of changing twenties, tens and fives into pocketfuls of singles for use ashore as taxi or ricksha fares, tips, bribes or minor purchases. Those disappeared forever and a chronic dollar-bill shortage plagued every world-cruise purser. No matter how many were stacked in the safe when *Franconia* departed from New York, by Singapore supplies ran so low they had to be replenished from banks ashore.

Franconia steamed north to the Chinese mainland. Although the Japanese were already pillaging Manchuria, those northern battles remained remote from *Franconia*'s tourist trains snaking inland from Hong Kong to Canton. But one rail journey had to be curtailed, a long excursion north from Shanghai to Mukden, then east and south the length of the Korean peninsula to Pusan where a ferry would carry those temporary rail travellers to Yokohama and reunion with *Franconia*. War ruled out that overland journey in 1937 just as North Korean intransigency prevents it today.

Nevertheless, *Franconia*'s far-eastern ports provided, as always, a splendid finale to her longest cruise. That year, the film version of *Lost Horizon* had been released and Shangri-La was every passenger's dream, although perhaps it was really to be

" THREE   JOLLY   SAILORS "

Three Jolly Cunard tars from the twenties. Although apparently frisky here, the first-line vessels were beginning to show their age. (The University Archives, The University of Liverpool)

found on board *Franconia* herself. But in addition to fantasy, ironic portents abounded. Sailing out of Manila in early April, Americans gathered along the rail to glimpse the fortress island of Corregidor, a name that only a few years later would resonate as a symbol of defeat and despair. As if to underscore the irony, ship's lecturer Charles Batchelder assembled his passengers one Pacific evening to discuss 'Must Japan expand in Asia?' Weeks earlier, he had offered his audience 'Will Europe go democratic, communist or fascist?' And who among those well-fed, contented passengers could know that the vessel on which they were accommodated so comfortably would, grey-painted, serve as Churchill's wartime headquarters at Yalta?

A combined lassitude and naïveté typifies every

cruise passenger-load; it stems from territorial limitation and the 1937 Franconian mood proved no exception. 'Innocents abroad', they were Americans at play – well off, curious, good natured and generous to a fault, but detached by their special circumstances from any consideration of world events. Their most enthusiastic involvement with matters beyond the ship's railings came on 12 May, Coronation Day. All the passengers watched as the entire ship's company, drawn up on the boat deck, toasted King George VI's accession to the throne abandoned by his older brother half a year earlier.

The final irony was that Japan and the Japanese enchanted them. What so appealed were the islands' exotic isolation and their inhabitants' exquisite manners and dedicated ingenuity. Never mind that, overseas, Japanese regiments had begun that fearful expansionist march that would end, catastrophically, in the nuclear rubble of Hiroshima. In 1937, Japan served as the world cruise's fitting apogee, the final far-eastern indulgence before the Americans returned to their side of the Pacific. Japan's seductive hospitality seemed to start far offshore as brightly illuminated fishing boats garlanded with light and glittering through the night appeared, like *barettes des diamants* in a jeweller's window, scattered invitingly over the velvet sea.

On Yokohama's passenger pier, a smartly dressed brass band played Sousa beneath *Franconia*'s packed promenade, drawn up in a crescent of folding chairs as though for a Sunday park concert. Behind them smiled a row of brilliantly clad women. Once the band's 'Stars and Stripes Forever' had thumped to a rousing conclusion, their female colleagues took centrestage, performing a sinuous dance of welcome, posturing delicately with fan and kimono hem – a weaving, waving choreography of welcome picking its way across the grimy, puddled concrete of the pier.

That reception encapsulated Japan's national spirit, the visored martial faces of the men juxtaposed against the gentle flowered silks of the women. It proved irresistible to Franconians who swarmed down the gangway, awkwardly acknowledging and returning the smiling bows that greeted them everywhere. But inland, a cultural fatigue overtook them. Sightseeing saturation had set in and earnest passengers relented from their earlier intentions to commit to memory or film every wonder that their eyes, and tired feet, could possibly absorb. Though the same carloads drew up at Tokyo or Kyoto shrines, though shoes were doffed and dusty buddhas inspected, there was a perceptible shift. There was a longing to exchange culturally impelled automobile for acquisitive ricksha, hurtling along the Ginza in search of yet another bolt of silk, more intriguing lacquerware or captivating jade and ivory. The prospect of home loomed as well and sobering selections remained to be made, obligatory keepsakes for friends, family and servants.

By then, *Franconia* was a floating marketplace itself, storage holds and cabins bursting with passenger loot from fanbacked Philippine chairs to Benares brass, from cloisonné urns to Indian carpets, all awaiting the awful day of reckoning on the pier. Some spoils had already gone on ahead, dispatched from long-past ports by obliging Thomas Cook men, crated, insured and shipped to the US or UK.

After Honolulu and before California, *Franconia*'s fragile cruise community braced for the end. West-

More fun and games 'crossing the line': spectators include passengers above, crew below. (The Ocean Liner Museum)

A sampler of Cunard playing cards from single-stackers to the Queens. (Peter Radmore collection)

coast passengers would disembark at Los Angeles's San Pedro piers, sparing themselves a transcontinental return trek from New York. The Starlight Theatre's final evocative evening performance was a gala one, the *Franconia Follies* – 'One Act and Fifteen Follies' – with a cast of 'frenzied, frantic Franconians'. The Franconian debs strutted 'A Mad Madagascar Moment' followed by 'Mood India'.

Afterwards, a perspiring Ross Skinner, still in greasepaint, galvanised his staff to award the committee's recommended prizes for bridge, for deck tennis, for shuffleboard and squash, for best spelling bee, for best general knowledge, for best-kept scrapbook, for best everything! Then the captain thanked all the committees and adjourned them *sine die*, or at least until the following January in New York.

Two days later, at San Pedro, the first immutable passenger defection began. A signed menu that remains in one passenger scrapbook betrays the regret on board: 'We were in the hope that when the Riff-Raff left us in San Pedro, we would get to bed nights but it still goes on.' In truth, it did not still go on. The pace slowed as *Franconia* continued through the Caribbean and up into the Atlantic. The awful business of dismantling that long cabin tenancy was begun. Trunks, crates and parcels were packed, tagged and assembled by hardworking stewards along the portside promenade. There were farewell drinks, farewell dinners and giggling farewells late at night between junior officers and some of the younger lady passengers.

Then Manhattan, last seen in January's bitter cold, arose over the horizon, wreathed in benevolent spring warmth. The world cruise was over. Captain Dolphin brought his ship alongside Pier 54 and rang down 'Finished with Engines'. Far below, Chief Engineer Cuttle logged that the vessel's twin shafts had completed over 10 million revolutions in propelling patient, comfortable *Franconia* more than 35,000 nautical miles (64,860km).

The anticipatory approach from home to pier was reversed. Front halls were re-achieved, family and friends reunited, everything unwrapped and unpacked, mountains of mail and magazines sorted through, domestic routine resumed. But long after the brass rims of cloisonné souvenirs had tarnished, long after central heating had split tropical bamboo, long after ivory sculpture had gathered its first home dust on the mantelpiece, the memory of those *Franconia* months 'chasing sunshine and happiness' would endure. The time when a turn around the stern promenade deck with its pungent reek of funnel smoke was miraculously supplanted, walking forward, by a mystical tropical fragrance wafting over the bows, would never be forgotten.

A vision to cherish: Franconia *at rest off the Seychelles.* (The Ocean Liner Museum)

417 SEYCHELLES

THE FIRST TROOPS
WITH CUNARD

It is not very comfortable in a troopship, shut up with scarcely standing room, constantly being pitched and tossed about.

> Anonymous notes from a
> Crimean soldier

Damn the men, look after the horses!

> A corporal in the Imperial Yeomanry
> bound for the Boer War

When we think of Cunarders carrying troops overseas to battle, we almost invariably picture the giant Queens of World War II. Images come to mind of those familiar, grey-painted monsters steaming out of New York bound for Gourock, Cunard's wartime Scottish terminus, open decks crammed with GIs. *Queen Mary* and *Queen Elizabeth* thundered alone across a hostile Atlantic under which lurked history's largest submarine fleet, the torpedo not only their weapon of necessity but their weapon of choice as well. The U-boat's most potent armament enjoyed the most favourable tactical odds. Whereas ashore, thousands of rounds of small-arms ammunition might be required to stop a platoon or hundreds of artillery shells needed to dislodge a dug-in battalion, a single well-placed torpedo striking the *Queen Mary* would have put paid to an entire division. The risks entailed in transporting troops overseas during both world wars were appalling, but in World War II a submerged U-boat lucky enough to have sunk one of the Queens would have dealt a crippling blow to the Allies' logistical capability as well as destroyed

one of the two most valuable merchant vessels in the world.

In contrast, England's nineteenth-century soldiers steamed off to war with relative impunity. Since their enemies offered no naval opposition on the high seas, fleets of Cunarders including *Niagara, Jura, Simla* and *Cambria* sailed under charter to Her Majesty's government; in fact such was the drain on Cunard's resources that the North Atlantic service was temporarily returned to a fortnightly series of departures. Sailings from port were festive rather than furtive with bands playing 'The Girl I Left Behind Me' and hundreds of spectators crowding the pier. Masters never had to black out their ships, sail in convoy or seek the protection of escorting warships. Seen from over the water, early trooping Cunarders were indistinguishable from peacetime Cunarders, save during the Boer War when large white numerals adorned the liners' sides to help identify them from afar within Table Bay's crowded anchorage.

Aquitania steams into New York Harbour after the outbreak of war in September 1939. She had been painted grey all over her superstructure. (Left) Her lifeboats were carried swung out throughout the entire crossing.

Homebound from Balaklava: British artillery units and their horses being loaded on board for the return to Blighty. The hulk Medora *is used as a loading barge for the larger* Argo. (Illustrated London News)

EMBARKATION OF ARTILLERY ON BOARD THE "ARGO," AT BALACLAVA, FOR ENGLAND—SKETCHED BY R. LANDELLS—(SEE NEXT PAGE)

As a result of his invaluable contribution to the Crimean War, Samuel Cunard was knighted by a grateful queen. He had delivered his vessels into government service willingly and with exemplary dispatch. He was able to do so, quite simply, because so little conversion was involved. Regimental officers slept two to a cabin, as though booked for a peacetime Atlantic crossing. Indeed, in those casual days, long before the emergence of ruthless shipboard billeting authorities, matters of space were settled quite differently; two officers who found a carpenter installing a third temporary bunk in their cabin ordered him to take it apart, pack up his tools and get out! But their men, who slung hammocks in berthing compartments, shared the lower decks with additional involuntary wartime occupants – four-legged ones. The embarkation and accommodation of hundreds of cavalry mounts characterised every Crimean and Boer trooping voyage. Additional stores were loaded onto the troopships as well – bales of fodder, saddlery, field rations, weapons and, always put on gingerly last of all, ammunition.

Alas, horses do not take kindly to rough seas, no more than many of their masters. Since they are pathologically unable to vomit, whatever miseries humans suffer from seasickness are doubly distressing for horses. Perhaps that explained their inherent reluctance to go on board. On one occasion it took nearly an hour for six sweating troopers to coax a single stubborn mare across the equine gangway connecting *Jura*'s cargo port with Portsmouth's dock.

Horses were stabled on board wherever room could be found, either in temporary stalls on deck or far below; but not always very far down in the hull. Even though subsequent Ministry of Transport regulations prohibited the practice of stabling horses above men, often in the mid-nineteenth century no such sanitary precautions were observed. Troops and horses were berthed and stabled, respectively, in whatever configuration most suited.

In addition to seasickness, horses suffered from successive maritime agonies during passage to Balaklava. The worst were storm and heat. On one Cunarder, 317 horses clattered on board to accompany 391 officers and men. Once the vessel had cleared Spithead, it steamed into a gale roaring up-Channel. Everyone on board was sick, the men describing the 'heavers' at the rail, the officers suggesting that 'the swell discomposed some of our stomachs'. The horses felt it worse, 'all snorting and tumbling about', recorded a cavalry officer. They were confined in purposely tight stalls, additionally supported by belly-bands designed to help them keep their footing. Two of the on-deck animals died during passage across the Bay of Biscay, their carcases hurled over the side. Those stabled below fared better at first, being lower in the hull and out of the weather, but their turn came later in the Mediterranean. The July heat was appalling and there were more equine fatalities, especially among those stabled near the engine spaces. Two horses on deck were driven literally mad by the heat and had to be destroyed. Whenever the ship rolled, the animals continually tried to keep their spines level, forever bending or stretching their legs; once ashore, they could not be ridden for days. Horses were not the only fatalities that trip; a private soldier went to sleep on the edge of the open engine-room hatch and fell to his death in the engines.

All soldiers who 'took the Queen's shilling' and

sailed to war in the nineteenth century did so to the accompanying whinny of sick or frightened mounts as well as the noisome reek of the stables whenever lower-deck stalls were mucked out and tubs of manure manhandled topside to be emptied over the rail. How did the soldiers fare? Spared the inconvenience of blackouts and life preservers obligatory for their twentieth-century successors, they were confined instead to many more days at sea. The fastest ships steamed from Portsmouth to Balaklava in sixteen days; slow vessels consumed as much as three weeks.

Officers enjoyed first-class perks, sailing in regular cabin accommodation; through contacts with their opposite numbers on board, they managed to make themselves quite comfortable. One officer wrote to his wife from the *Jura* in 1854: 'The purser has made my cabin very cozy by putting up

Queen Elizabeth 2's only hull colour change appeared just after August 1982 when, following her Falkland service, she appeared briefly with a pale grey hull. Within a few months, she went back to charcoal grey. (Cunard)

Queen Elizabeth 2

some hatpins on which I can lay my things. He has also had my lamp fixed up, and given me a looking glass.' He concluded his first letter home thanking his wife for the scrap of carpet she had thoughtfully included in his bedding; it was a great help on the *Jura*'s bare cabin floor and would be even more useful in the cold of the Crimea.

On *Simla*, another officer's verdict on shipboard conditions reads like a passenger testimonial from a crossing: 'The cook was capital, the food abundant. We enjoyed champagne and claret twice weekly.' Officers dined in the ship's saloon, each meal preceded by a token tasting of the men's rations hastened up from the mess deck by one of the sergeants. After lunch, passenger/officers sprawled beneath awnings rigged against the Mediterranean sun aft on the quarterdeck 'reading, smoking and enjoying ourselves'. Training sessions were enlivened by hanging bottles and tins in the rigging for target practice; an occasional frolicking porpoise served as well. (Target shooting from the decks of a troopship remains a commonplace diversion to the present. When *Queen Elizabeth 2* was en route to the Falklands, an enthusiastic Guards' machine gunner left his mark on the foc's'le-head railing – one of his armour-piercing rounds punched a hole clean through it. It has been preserved as a Falkland battle memento.)

The men's meals were less appealing than the officers'. Then as now, food on board ship remained topic one. Complained one private soldier: 'There was not enough food and not enough water.' Officers and men alike were restricted to 3 quarts (3.4 litres) a day each for shaving, washing and drinking. Curiously, no sail or canvas pool was ever rigged on any Crimean trooper. The men were fed a version of Cunard's stolid transatlantic fare:

cocoa and biscuit for breakfast, pea soup and salt pork for lunch, salt beef and 'pudding' for dinner and more biscuits and tea at dusk. The only late evening collation was a dram of rum as though they were in the trenches.

There was no seaman's slop chest from which additional food could be purchased but there were bumboats at ports along the way. Off Gibraltar, troops lined the ship's railings to buy 'oranges, figs, tobacco, very good bread and very bad cheese'. Gibraltar was the first stop, although no one went ashore, and Malta the next, seven days after having left England. Once again, none of the men went ashore there because the barracks were too crowded to billet any more personnel. So the officers landed while their men endured yet another confining stay in port with the added unpleasantness of having their vessel coaled. The unceasing parade of Maltese bumboats that fought their way between the coal barges offered inferior food at rascally prices. The soldiers' only other diversion was throwing coins overboard, which clamoring boys dived after in the pristine depths of the harbour.

Officers ashore fared better. One went into business as a far-sighted wine merchant, buying up cases of claret at 12s a dozen; later, in the Crimea, he did a brisk trade at 100 per cent. He branched out into tea as well, but the price was discouraging. During her stopover at Malta, the *Europa* burned, stranding the Inniskillings there. Small detachments of the regiment were embarked on each successive troopship calling at the port, whenever room could be found for them.

The troopships sailed through the eastern Mediterranean and into the Bosphorus. Although once again no one went ashore, the offshore verdict about Constantinople in the 1850s was 'filthy'.

Postwar Cunarders ready for resumption of peacetime service. The date is 27 August, 1946. Queen Mary, on the left, is about to depart for New York, Aquitania is at right. Workers repair rail lines along the Southampton docks. Both vessels have their peacetime funnel colours back up although the hulls remain grey.

There was another bunkering stop at the Rumanian port of Varna and then, final destination, the tiny, crowded harbour at Balaklava. Ranks of sailing steamers, both cargo and passenger, were packed gunwhale to gunwhale along the front. Inbound troopships, already low on water and rations, often had to lie offshore for days on end awaiting their turn to dock and unload. A bleak hint of things to come accompanied those waits: the rumble of guns from Sebastopol was unceasing and the night sky flared with the light of battle.

Half a century later, Cunard Line vessels were dragooned for war again, this time to defeat the Boers in South Africa. Overall, it was a much larger operation, involving more men and material on board larger vessels; 'one of the most gigantic military movements undertaken', proclaimed the *Illustrated London News* with understandable jingoistic pride. The First Army Corps sailed from Southampton on 14 October 1899, reaching Cape Town by the end of the month. Achieving South Africa was, logistically, far more straightforward than the Crimea had been. Cape Town was the destination of every Union Castle Line steamer so there was less dependence on so many chartered Cunarders than there had been for the remote obscurity of the Black Sea. In addition to chartered troopships, Union Castle liners carried large contingents of soldiers on regularly scheduled sailings. Once, on *Tantallon Castle*, several enlisted men of the Duke of Cambridge's own company of the Imperial Yeomanry had private means enough to book first-class passage, berthing and dining incongruously with their colonels and majors.

But for most Boer War soldiers, conditions were only slightly improved from half a century earlier. One corporal wrote home an abbreviated critique of the on-board commissariat: 'Bad coffee, good porridge, inferior meat, detestable water, sometimes pudding edible only with famine appetite.' There was, by the turn of the century, a troop canteen on board at which soldiers could at least supplement their rations with sweets, bloater paste or tinned meats. The ships coaled at Las Palmas and the ubiquitous bumboats appeared beneath the railings once more, a floating market that dispensed oranges, bananas, eggs, tobacco and cigars. The coaling was trying. 'Everything aft of the funnels', wrote one begrimed trooper, 'was coated with an eighth of an inch of coal dust.'

Farther south, the heat on board became intolerable. One shipload of 2,000 guardsmen travelled all the way to Cape Town wearing their scarlet tunics and black trousers. But there was relief for twenty men at a time in the sail bath, a temporary canvas pool that, by the turn of the century, was rigged on all liners passing through the tropics. The crossing the line ceremony, seldom a regular feature of transatlantic Cunarders, was improvised as a heaven-sent break in the monotony of the daily routine. Sailors doused grateful initiates into Neptune's domain with fire hoses.

But apart from that special geographical milestone, the men had to amuse themselves in very much the same way as their grandchildren and great grandchildren would on board *Aquitania* or the Queens forty years later. There were sing-songs, there was a ship's newspaper, there were marathon card games in every corner above and below decks, there was the laundering of clothes and, occasionally, the inspection of kit. Whenever enough spare deckspace could be cleared, regimental boxing matches were fought on deck, bouts similar to those that would take place on board passenger vessels between the wars. One vital activity took place aft: military surgeons set up a makeshift clinic on the stern and administered typhoid inoculations to every man on board. So to the heat and boredom and seasickness was added a sometimes feverish recovery from reaction to the shots.

Although wireless had still not appeared on board, communication with England was in many cases vastly improved over that of either world war. GIs embarking for Europe were not allowed to tell their families on the eve of embarkation either the name of their ship or their destination. But troopers bound for South Africa could, and did, tell all; moreover, their uncensored letters often reached England before they reached Cape Town. Every northbound steamer encountered on the voyage stopped obligingly to transfer precious mail bags on board for passage home to Blighty.

The weather relented, the seas roughened and imminent landfall at Cape Town was heralded, as always, by the apparition of Cape pigeons over the bows. Table Bay, although larger than Balaklava, was just as crowded with the press of wartime tonnage; hence the identifying numerals painted on all troopships' flanks. One officer suggested that Table Bay seemed like 'a permanent naval review'. Once again, as in the Crimea, such was the logistical crush ashore that freshly arrived troopships often waited at anchor for days before disembarking the men. The latter would then proceed either on foot or by waggon in dusty columns to the seething turmoil of the Castle at Camp Maitland for processing and dispatch to the front.

Months or years later, soldiers embarked for their homeward passage. The names of some would be missing from the regimental rolls, some would be wounded or maimed but all who had survived craved the sight of green England once more and the embrace of wives, parents or children. Then the chartered ships, discharged from government service, returned north to Liverpool for dry docking, cleaning and repainting. *Umbria, Aurania, Servia, Pavonia* and *Catalonia* were reprovisioned for peacetime service. *Carinthia* and *Sylvania* had been employed on the New Orleans–Cape Town run, transporting horses and mules to South Africa. Once again, Cunard's full complement of ships would steam out of the Mersey for New York. The company's transatlantic strength had been returned to normal.

But a crucial precedent had been established – first instance of Cunarders enrolled for war, of Cunard passengers embarking with rifle and pack rather than steamer trunk and valise. Those early trooping voyages were forerunners of dozens to come in the ensuing decades of the twentieth century. Long lines of soldiers would clamber through the sides of the great grey liners. They would spend a week or more suspended in a watery limbo between ports, enduring the same ordeal the emigrants knew of heaving seas, cramped berthing compartments, short commons, drear sea days, seasickness and misery. At crossing's end was the sweet prospect – at Gourock, Suez, Sidney or, homebound, Manhattan – of disembarkation and the end of that crowded, unforgettable episode of their war, packed below deck on a blacked-out Cunarder.

The real question is whether so large a vessel and so elaborate a masterpiece is really needed to convey passengers across the Atlantic. The possibilities of the vessel being an economic failure have to be faced.

Extract from a *Times* editorial of 1930 about the proposed *Queen Mary*

The forces of ignorance and stupidity ranged against you were and still are formidable yet there she is, the best thing (in my opinion) that we in this country have produced for years. Of course, this is wrong and that could have been better, we all know that. Hugh Casson thinks she is the best ever.

Letter from Jon Bannenberg to Dennis Lennon about *Queen Elizabeth 2*

Periodically, interspersed between crossings, world cruises and Caribbean forays, *Queen Elizabeth 2* sails out of Southampton and back for what her crew call 'teapot cruises'. These are designed for, and booked heavily by, Britons; drinks prices are lowered, menus revised and entertainment geared to specific British tastes. In one sense, teapot cruises represent a fleeting and, for many Americans, sorely missed aspect of Cunard's yesterday; they summon up the company's staunch, no-nonsense Liverpool and Southampton roots, a time when its image no less than its vessels were peculiarly and indubitably British.

If a City of London stockbroker were to sell shares in *QE2* teapot cruises, he would doubtless call them Empire Preferred. Queens *Mary* and *Elizabeth* were operated on a solid Empire Preferred basis, teapot ships *primus inter pares*.

Of course, I am biased by age and background. As a Scots-American, my British half remembers only too well the London of my childhood – lamp-lit, fire-lit, sometimes fogbound London, seat of Empire, staid, ordered and placid. It is another city now, a metamorphosis reflected, perforce, in the tenor of its life and its inhabitants as well. Britons have turned their backs on so much of their traditional but perhaps no longer workable past. It is a saddening state of affairs which distresses thousands of Cunard's oldest American friends; but we remain less distressed by what has been rejected than by what has been improvised in its place.

Queen Elizabeth 2 has survived as a microcosm of that new Britain. An early, spurious modernism, now happily relinquished, suffused the vessel at the time of her fitting out. Ashore, the 'swinging sixties' prevailed, led by 'swinging London', and there was a misguided attempt to implement that populist dream on board. 'Ships', lamented the copy from one Cunard campaign of the period, 'have been boring long enough', a curiously masochistic admission from a company that had previously prided itself on exemplary tradition.

The first *QE2* stewards were issued turtle-necked shirts instead of collars and ties, and there was a determined attempt to weed out the old and bring in the new, from passengers to personnel. Colonel Blimp was out, Carnaby Street was in. I can still remember the bemused scorn of Bob, veteran barman from *Caronia*, *Mauretania*, *Queen Mary* and

(Left) Queen Mary's farewell and finish: Cunard's grand old ship sails out of New York for the last time in 1967. (Below) She is tied up today in Long Beach, California, as a combined hotel, museum and exhibition centre. Hyatt and then Wrather have handed the custodial torch to Disney. (William Batchelder)

(Left) *The first model of* Queen Elizabeth 2. (Dennis Lennon)

(Above) *Eight years later, additional cabins are added for the second time.* (Cunard)

Queen Elizabeth, when asked by a keen but very junior company planner if he were capable of remaining on his feet for as long as ten hours. 'Eighteen is more like it', was his imperturbable response.

In retrospect, the company may be forgiven their anxiety to wipe the slate clean. *Queen Elizabeth 2*'s design impact was significant, a breath of fresh, naval architectural air. Dennis Lennon, dean of Britain's interior designers, had overseen a design effort that marshalled disparate tastes and concepts under one comprehensive umbrella. His was not an easy task: storms were frequent, resignations commonplace and company obfuscation occasionally confounding. But the result, nursed down the

Clyde and steaming proudly into Southampton after years of toil, was stunning.

Sir Colin Anderson wrote to Lennon: 'Every prospect pleases. I don't remember ever going around a ship with such continuing pleasure.' Lord Snowdon wired: 'What you have personally achieved with *QE2* makes one proud to be British. The overall creative design, the meticulous detailing and simple honest sophistication combined with change of pace and mood is breathtaking.' When renderings and maquettes of the new Cunarder's interiors were unveiled in the Haymarket's Design Centre, *The Times* shipping correspondent hailed the look as 'bright, crisp and gay'.

The Financial Times went even further. Bewitched by what it perceived as a new crossing/cruising parlay, Arthur Sandles predicted novel employment for the new vessel. His words read rather quaintly after the fact:

There are signs that even the North Atlantic run, traditional heart of Cunard passenger business, may be in for a revival, particularly if Cunard can develop a long-trip southerly route business which could take Southampton–New York passengers via the sunshine of the Canaries and the Caribbean . . . The *QE2* could fly between Southampton, Le Havre and New York by way of Lisbon, the Canaries, the Caribbean and Miami, taking about 15 days on the whole voyage. The southern route, as it is called, would tap the growing market for sea holidays as distinct from straightforward transportation.

Lloyd's Register was as laudatory as it was cautionary: 'The most luxurious – and expensive – passenger ship in the world.'

(Main picture) *Glistening under the lights,* Queen Elizabeth 2, *as yet unnamed, taking shape on the ways at John Brown's yard.* (Cunard)

(Inset) QE2 *takes the water for the first time, plunging into the Clyde; the drag chains are slowing down the giant ship's rearward surge.* (Dennis Lennon)

With such overwhelmingly positive feedback, small wonder that Cunard opted for a clean break with the past, finished with teapot forever save for the occasional insular outing. Shares of Empire Preferred were liquidated in favour of massive investments in International Acceptables. The company's change in strategy coincided with America's cruise infatuation that began in the 1970s and continues unabated to the present. The new ship and its new philosophy were positioned admirably to take advantage of waves of new passengers.

There are two kinds of fools, those who think that everything old is good and those who think that everything new is better. Perhaps Cunard might better have compromised with their past rather than reject it out of hand. The question begs an answer: how to retain a company's traditional shipboard flavour while at the same time spicing it with contemporary seasoning?

The gastronomic simile is apropos. Herewith a sampling from a 1933 *Berengaria* menu: 'Cambridge Sausages, Oxford–Leicester Brawn, Derby Round of Beef, Veal and Ham Pie, Compote of Fruit and Custard, Carlton Dates, Assorted Berengaria Confections and Canapes Edward VII.' Cunard passengers steaming across the North Atlantic between the wars were plugged into the vessel's country of origin, paid handsome dividends from a portfolio of Empire Preferred. The ship, its owners, its nationality and its passenger offerings were perceived as synonymous.

Compare that Cunard menu of half a century ago to a selection from Cunard's *Sea Goddess I* today: 'Hearts of Iceberg with Buttermilk Garlic Dressing, Ravioli (with) Creamy Herb Sauce, Lobster and Conch Gazpacho, Surf and Turf 'Nouvelle' and Grapefruit Campari Sherbet.' What a break with

Her Majesty Queen Elizabeth examines a model of one of the ship's outdoor pools with Dennis Lennon. (Dennis Lennon)

the past, what wide-ranging, almost playful experimentation! But, alas, where, amongst all that International Acceptable, is England and where Cunard?

Of course, it is not lost on me that whereas *Berengaria* was crossing, *Sea Goddess* is cruising; nor that it seems axiomatic that contemporary cruise-speak transforms tradition into trend, on-board shops into boutiques, passengers into guests and cabins into suites. But in that inevitable process, certain honest perceptions about the vessel and its origins have been blurred. Should ships capitalise on their nationality or try and suppress it?

In the past, a sense of history always prevailed, not only on British and American liners but on their continental rivals as well. Norddeutscher–Lloyd

(Above left) *One of QE2's endearing breakfast perquisites: 'jam boys' in the dining rooms bring a trolley-full of marmalade to your table, dispensed from Empire Preferred jars rather than those ghastly little International Acceptable plastic packets.*

(Above right) *Montague Dawsons's study of* Mauretania *at Liverpool.* (Cunard)

(Left) *Captain Alan Bennell at his desk, coping with the demanding job of running* Queen Elizabeth 2.

ships epitomised Potsdam afloat, so much so that their Hanseatic colleagues of the Hamburg–Amerika Linie adopted a Gallic look instead – seagoing Louis Seize; but both emphasised brass bands and Strauss. Swedish-American ships were exhilaratingly Scandinavian and raised the level of mid-ocean smörgåsbord to a fine art. Paquebots of the French Line, boasting 'the longest gangplank in the world', assured boarding passengers, in effect, that they were embarking into the very heart of France, its culture and decorative arts. Holland–American ships to the present relish their Dutch-ness, a carefully cultivated decorative synthesis of tulip, delft, pewter and seventeenth-century maritime glory.

At rest in New York,
seen from astern: QE2
sports a new and more substantial
funnel after her re-engining from
a steam turbine to a diesel-electric
vessel.

But one contemporary exception seems typical of a worrisome new trend. Japan's Mitsubishi Company, owners of the historic NYK Line, entered the cruise market in the late eighties. They chose the name Crystal Cruises and situated their headquarters in southern California. During their formative days, the owners approached Dennis Lennon with the suggestion that he take on some of their first vessel's public rooms. Lennon was intrigued at the prospect of recreating a Japanese Pacific look from between the wars. But Mitsubishi demurred: their vessels, they pointed out firmly, were to have no inkling of Japan or the Japanese, nothing more far eastern than Hawaii. Regretfully, Lennon bowed out of the project. Was Mitsubishi merely trying to forget Pearl Harbor or, more likely, was it convinced that shipboard success today demands conformity?

On *QE2* today, the same move, from nationalism to internationalism, seems as implacable as it may be inevitable. During luncheon in the first-class restaurants, dining-room captains distribute advance copies of that evening's menu to every table, soliciting special orders at the same time. As ever, most Cunard passengers are American and most of their special orders reflect our national preoccupation with that awful provincial catch-phrase 'gourmet dining': duck à l'orange, beef Wellington and, for dessert, predictably, crêpes Suzette or cerises flambées.

But if I am on board, when congenial Norman Broadbent approaches me in the Queen's Grill with order pad at the ready, he is prepared for a nostalgic orgy of Empire Preferred: shepherd's pie, steak and kidney pudding, kedgeree, cold roast beef with pickled walnuts and, for a sweet, treacle tart or plum duff. Though the portions, when they arrive, are heroic, judging from covetous glances from adjacent stewards, leftovers will find ready takers beyond the green baize door.

But too often, Norman advises me, British special orders are increasingly hard to fulfil. During summer crossings in 1988, only one Queen's Grill sous-chef was prepared to tackle steak and kidney; the chef that crossing was Swiss, and Empire Preferred had been eclipsed by International Acceptables.

Perhaps it should not be surprising that Britishness is waning throughout Cunard's fleet. The majority of those seven hulls originated under foreign management. *Sagafjord, Vistafjord* and both *Sea Goddesses* sprang from Norwegian concepts. *Cunard Countess* and *Princess*, which ply Caribbean, Panamanian and Alaskan waters exclusively, were built to Cunard order but have been adapted to cruise conventions far removed from the company's North Atlantic origins. So *QE2* rests in splendid isolation, the company's only real link with its past. As such, one hopes she will retain her historic ties, and that Americans will be greeted on board by Cunard's venerable and evocative continuum.

Can, or should, the clock be turned back? I think it boils down to a matter of image and intent, whether to adapt to conventional expectations or strive to duplicate the best from Cunard's past? Surely it should be the latter. Americans who were lifelong devotees of *Mauretania* and *Aquitania*, Americans who embarked for months at sea on board *Franconia* and *Caronia*, Americans who thronged both Queens throughout these buoyant postwar years, will always be attracted by a time-tested formula rather than bland cruising universality.

A significant menu cover marking the last Cunard vessel's relinquishment of steam in favour of the ubiquitous diesel. (Cunard Line)

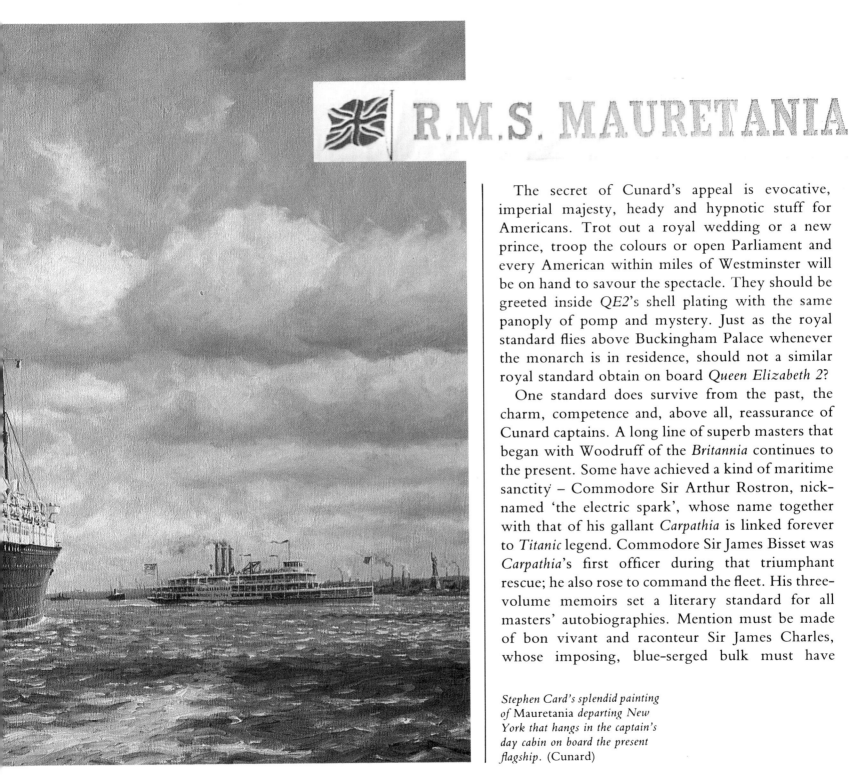

R.M.S. MAURETANIA

The secret of Cunard's appeal is evocative, imperial majesty, heady and hypnotic stuff for Americans. Trot out a royal wedding or a new prince, troop the colours or open Parliament and every American within miles of Westminster will be on hand to savour the spectacle. They should be greeted inside *QE2*'s shell plating with the same panoply of pomp and mystery. Just as the royal standard flies above Buckingham Palace whenever the monarch is in residence, should not a similar royal standard obtain on board *Queen Elizabeth 2*?

One standard does survive from the past, the charm, competence and, above all, reassurance of Cunard captains. A long line of superb masters that began with Woodruff of the *Britannia* continues to the present. Some have achieved a kind of maritime sanctity – Commodore Sir Arthur Rostron, nick-named 'the electric spark', whose name together with that of his gallant *Carpathia* is linked forever to *Titanic* legend. Commodore Sir James Bisset was *Carpathia*'s first officer during that triumphant rescue; he also rose to command the fleet. His three-volume memoirs set a literary standard for all masters' autobiographies. Mention must be made of bon vivant and raconteur Sir James Charles, whose imposing, blue-serged bulk must have

Stephen Card's splendid painting of Mauretania *departing New York that hangs in the captain's day cabin on board the present flagship.* (Cunard)

119

haunted *Aquitania*'s bridge to the end. Captains Sir Edgar Britten, Donald MacLean and Harry Grattidge stay in the mind as well, as does Captain Eric Ashton-Irvine who, retired from the company, became a fellow-adopted New Yorker.

But most Cunard masters retire to gentle Hampshire, either inland in some quiet backwater or within Southampton itself, hard by the city-port from which they sailed so many times. How familiar are those recent masters: the beaming, ruddy face of Bill Law; jovial, white-thatched Treasure Jones; the languid urbanity of Geoffrey Marr, not only at sea during the 'Lizzie's' last years but during her tragic Floridian twilight as well. A treasured sight is Bill Warwick one Christmas afternoon, alone on the port bridge wing, scanning the sky through binoculars for seabirds as *QE2* slid down the coast of Martinique. What about Mortimer Hehir's gruff, jocular laugh and the bluff cordiality of Bob Arnott, whose foggy, mid-ocean birthday I once helped celebrate with some hasty doggerel which he was kind enough to include in his memoirs? And dark, dapper, piano-playing Peter Jackson, one of *QE2*'s two Falkland masters, fresh back from that extraordinary southern journey; at tea in his cabin, he showed me the kukri his Gurkha passengers had given him and cautioned me, as he had been cautioned, never to draw it from its scabbard unless intent on using it. Then there is the present commodore of the fleet, Doug Ridley, whose ready grin and cheerful face have long been *QE2* crossing concomitants. And finally, immensely tall, basso profundo Lawrence Portet, a striking figure of command under whose firm hand *QE2* rode out hurricane Gloria during a memorable autumn crossing in 1985.

In the summer of 1987, Alan Bennell was serving

A QE2 menu cover.

— is the —
INTERNATIONAL
WORLD
— of the —
QUEEN
ELIZABETH 2

as general manager on board *Cunard Princess* in Alaskan waters. A telex from company president Ralph Bahna requested his immediate presence at North American headquarters in New York. Expecting, as he later recounted, 'a rocket of some sort', he appeared in the president's office at the appointed hour. Bahna invited him in, closed the door and then took off his jacket. Bennell's spirits sank. But he was as surprised as he was delighted when Bahna proposed: 'How would you like to drive the *Queen*?' It was for Alan Bennell, as for all his predecessors, the pinnacle of a long career. He was no stranger to the vessel, in fact I had met him on board years earlier as staff captain before his transfer to both *Countess* and *Princess*. Now he was back on board the flagship with the coveted rank of master.

He seems extraordinarily well chosen for the job. Every QE2 cruise or crossing starts with a ritual the second night out, known on board as the captain's handshake. After two consecutive evenings have elapsed, every passenger on board has met and been photographed with the master. Those pictures are prized, cherished mementos of the shipboard experience. Most captains tackle the chore briskly, clasping hands and smiling in perfect synchronisation with the photographer's flash, then passing the passenger adroitly along to the cruise director before turning to the next couple. Though the greeting is warm, the turnover is rapid; by eight o'clock, the line is finished and the Queen's Room is full of passengers, all of whom have shaken the master's hand.

But Alan Bennell is notorious for extending each passenger encounter extravagantly. Not for him a perfunctory assembly-line greeting; the picture taken, Bennell launches into a long cordial exchange with each passenger that sometimes stretches into precious minutes as the patient queue stretches in turn across the Queen's Room and out along the portside corridor. Indeed, Bennell's loquacity is the despair of hotel managers and chief stewards; by eight o'clock, when he is brought centrestage for his obligatory remarks to the assembled company, dozens of passengers have still not reached his side. But they will not be forgotten. Bennell always schedules a supplementary handshake the following night, until he has chatted up every passenger on board.

He is equally conscientious during his cocktail parties with a congenial mix of passengers from both sides of the Atlantic. The master's day cabin is high in the ship and, if the weather is rough, one feels the motion. The women are in long dresses and the men in black tie; QE2 is the last vessel in the world where, as in the old days, one dresses for dinner each night. The talk is loud and cheerful and drinks issue non-stop from the adjacent pantry. Bennell is everywhere, greeting newcomers at the door, topping up glasses, making introductions and never at a loss for engaging small talk.

The day after one such party, I had tea with him. Despite a staggering accumulation of paperwork on his desk and an unceasing incoming barrage of messages and telephone calls, Alan somehow found time not only to drink a cup of tea with me but to make it as well. I suggested to him that he obviously seemed to relish the sometimes burdensome social demands of his job, that his role as captain is one he fulfils with pleasure. He agreed and suggested, quite simply, that he feels honoured and privileged to have the post.

Queen Elizabeth 2 is lucky to have him. Perhaps the last of her kind, she is a ship to be cherished.

Under Alan Bennell's amiable captaincy, she sails triumphantly along, secure in his competent and caring hands. As he talked on the phone, I looked behind me at Montague Dawson's lovely canvas of *Mauretania*, her great bows at rest, looming above the Mersey's tug-smoke and mist. On the portside wall, larger still, is another *Mauretania*, a flawless study by Stephen Card, the man who painted the cover of this volume. It shows the 'Mary', as *Mauretania* was known by her crew, steaming downriver out of New York.

What perfect decoration for a Cunard master's cabin, *Mauretania* at either end of her transatlantic run, Cunard's Anglo-American connection linking England with America, linking old world with new, linking as well my Scottish–American origins. How fitting that the company's golden ship from the early years of this century should be remembered on board the company's golden ship at century's end. Long may she sail!

Cunard's great translatlantic parlay: Queen Elizabeth *by sea, Concorde by air.* (Cunard)

A broadside view of Queen Elizabeth 2 *by Dennis Lennon.*

1840: *Britannia*, first of four initial steamers, inaugurates Cunard's North American steam service from Liverpool to Halifax and Boston. Save for grounding in Halifax, the voyage is uneventful and record-breaking. *Columbia, Acadia* and *Caledonia* follow suit.

1847: Company's western terminus becomes New York instead: better communications inland and an ice-free harbour year-round among the advantages.

1848: Samuel Cunard and family move permanently to London.

1850: America's Collins Line steamer *Atlantic* enters service, eclipsing Cunard in speed and comfort alike.

1852: Cunarders *Andes* and *Alps*, the company's first iron hulls, screw propellers and emigrant quarters.

1854: The Crimean War breaks out and several Cunard vessels are withdrawn from Atlantic service for Black Sea trooping. The Collins Line makes further inroads.

1858: After loss of *Atlantic* (1854) and *Pacific* (1856), Collins Line collapses, ending threat to Cunard's Atlantic superiority.

1859: Samuel Cunard is knighted by a grateful Queen Victoria for his Crimean War service.

1863: *Scotia* sails, the last of Cunard's paddle-steamers.

1865: Sir Samuel Cunard dies at the age of 78.

1867: *Russia* enters service, a large screw steamer with service speed of 13 knots.

1880: The company goes public and its famous crowned lion with globe first appears. Disparaging rival tars dub it 'the monkey wi' the nut'.

1881: *Servia* debut – first steel hull and first Cunarder with electric lights.

1884: *Umbria* sails, the largest and fastest ship in the world and the company's first with mechanical refrigeration. The seven-day crossing becomes commonplace.

1885: *Umbria* is joined by sister *Etruria*. The new class boasts five decks and four commodious public rooms. The year previous, the company's vessels sailed five times the distance to the moon.

1894: *Lucania* and *Campania* enter service, larger still, with twin screws and hence pure steamers with no (backup) sails, only two bare pole masts.

1897: The two contrasting but inter-related events of that year were: Norddeutscher-Lloyd's *Kaiser Wilhelm der Grosse*'s capture of the Blue Ribbon and Charles Parsons's perfection of the marine steam turbine. His little *Turbinia* proved the shock/sensation of Her Majesty's Diamond Jubilee naval review at Spithead.

1900: Hamburg–Amerika Linie's *Deutschland* takes the Blue Ribbon in turn, yet another German triumph.

1901: *Campania* is the company's first ship to be equipped with a Marconi wireless and operators.

1905: *Carmania* and *Caronia* – 'the pretty sisters' – the first driven by steam turbines, the second by conventional reciprocating engines. The turbine proved economically superior.

1907: The debut of *Lusitania* and *Mauretania*, world's largest and fastest once again. The Blue Ribbon comes home.

1912: *Carpathia*, under command of Captain Arthur Rostron, en route from New York for a spring cruise in the Mediterranean, rescues 704 *Titanic* survivors and returns them to New York.

1914: *Aquitania* enters service, largest Cunarder to date. The war begins and one of the pretty sisters, now armed merchant cruiser *Carmania*, sinks the German liner *Cap Trafalgar*.

1915: *Lusitania* is sunk by a German U-boat. Over a thousand lives are lost and total sea war becomes a stark twentieth century reality.

1918: Hostilities end with November armistice. Cunard war losses total 22 vessels, 218,344 tons of shipping.

1921: *Berengaria*-ex-*Imperator* joins Cunard's postwar fleet; she and *Mauretania* and *Aquitania* make up the company's three-ship express service to New York.

1926: Captain Sir Arthur Rostron becomes fleet commodore.

1929: *Mauretania* loses Blue Ribbon to *Bremen*.

1930: Contract signed with John Brown's Yard for giant new Cunarder, hull number 534.

1931: Depression cash flow crisis halts shipyard work on hull 534. *Mauretania* painted white and sent cruising. Nine days from New York to the West Indies and back cost $130.

1934: Cunard and White Star join forces. Work on hull 534 resumes. Vessel launched that September, christened by Queen Mary with her name. *Berengaria* initiates Bermuda cruises out of New York, called the 'Bargain Area'.

1935: *Mauretania* withdrawn and cut up for scrap.

1936: *Queen Mary*'s maiden voyage to New York. Keel for her sister – hull 552 – laid down at John Brown's Yard.

1938: Christened by Queen Elizabeth with her name. *Berengaria* withdrawn from service. *Queen Mary* takes Blue Ribbon from *Normandie*.

1939: *Franconia* sails on last world cruise, the second *Mauretania* enters service and war breaks out in September. *Queen Mary* is stranded in New York. *Aquitania* starts war service.

1940: The company's centenary. *Queen Elizabeth* is spirited to New York under top secrecy. Later that year, both Queens are transformed into troopships.

1942: The Queens inaugurate their famous wartime Atlantic ferry service, carrying troops eastbound and wounded or prisoners of war westbound. After VE day, they bring home the GIs, then their brides and babies.

1946: *Queen Elizabeth*'s proper maiden voyage. The two-ship Queens' service, conceived in the late twenties, begins at last.

1948: *Caronia*, Cunard's epic cruise ship, enters service.

1950: *Aquitania* is withdrawn and scrapped, the only four-stacker to serve in both World Wars.

1957: Sinister transatlantic milestone: this year, for the first time, more passengers cross by air than by sea. The liners' decline begins.

1967: *Queen Mary* withdrawn after thirty-one years and sold to Long Beach, California, as hotel and tourist attraction, the most ambitious ocean liner preservation ever attempted.

1968: *Queen Elizabeth* retires to Florida, later sold to C. Y. Tung interests and towed to Hong Kong for conversion to *Seawise University* cruise ship. Upon completion, she burns and capsizes at anchor in Hong Kong harbour; sabotage is suspected but never proved.

1969: The Queens are dead, long live the *Queen!* *Queen Elizabeth 2* sails to New York on her maiden voyage.

1982: Summoned to war, *Queen Elizabeth 2* carries troops to South Georgia for the Falkland campaign and returns with wounded personnel. Inexplicably, her hull is temporarily painted pale grey for her return to the North Atlantic.

1983: Cunard takes over Norwegian American Cruises' *Sagafjord* and *Vistafjord*.

1985: Cunard absorbs Sea Goddess Cruises, bringing the fleet number to seven vessels.

1987: Converted from steam turbine to diesel-electric power, *Queen Elizabeth 2* undergoes a massive heart transplant and rework of her public rooms.

1990: The company's sesquicentennial celebration starts with *Queen Elizabeth 2*'s eastbound sailing on 17 July, 1990, from New York to Southampton. She is the only North Atlantic express liner left – what Cunard started, Cunard will finish.

Airlie, Mabell. *With the Guards We Shall Go* (Hodder & Stoughton, 1933)

Armstrong, Warren. *Atlantic Highway* (George G. Harrap & Co, 1961)

Arnott, Captain Robert Harry. *Captain of the Queen* (New English Library, 1982)

Bell, Major Sir George. *Soldier's Glory* (G. Bell & Sons, 1956)

Bisset, Sir James. *Sail Ho!* (Angus & Robertson, Sydney, 1958)

——. *Tramps and Ladies* (Angus & Robertson (UK) Ltd, 1959)

——. *Commodore* (Angus & Robertson (UK) Ltd, 1961)

——. *Ship Ahoy!* (Charles Birchall Ltd, nd)

Britten, Sir Edgar. *A Million Ocean Miles* (Hutchinson & Co, 1936)

Coleman, Terry. *The Liners* (Allen Lane, 1976)

de Kerbrech, Richard P. and Williams, David L. *Cunard White Star Liners of the 1930s* (Conway Maritime Press, 1988)

Fitzgibbon, Maurice. *Arts Under Arms* (Longmans Green and Co, 1901)

Franks, Henry. *Leaves from a Soldier's Note Book* (Mitre, 1979)

Fry, Henry. *History of North Atlantic Steam Navigation* (Sampson Low, 1896)

Grattidge, Captain Harry. *Captain of the Queens* (E. P. Dutton & Co, New York, 1956)

INDEX

Page numbers in *italic* denote illustrations

Johnson, Howard. *The Cunard Story* (Whittet Books, 1987)

Lacey, Robert. *The Queens of the North Atlantic* (Stein & Day, New York, 1976)

MacClean, Commodore Donald. *Queen's Company* (Hutchinson, 1965)

McNeil, Captain S. G. S. *In Great Waters* (Philip Allan & Co, 1932)

Marr, Geoffrey. *The Queens and I* (Adlard Coles, 1973)

Miller, William H. *Transatlantic Liners 1945–1980* (Arco Publishing Co, New York, 1981)

Potter, Neil and Frost, Jack. *The Mary* (George G. Harrap & Co, 1965)

— —. *The Elizabeth* (George G. Harrap & Co, 1961)

— —. *Queen Elizabeth 2* (George G. Harrap & Co, 1969)

Roche, T. W. E. *Samuel Cunard and the North Atlantic* (MacDonald, 1971)

Rolleston, Lady Maud. *Yeoman Service* (Smith Elder & Co, 1901)

Stevens, Leonard A. *The Elizabeth: Passage of a Queen* (Alfred A. Knopf, New York, 1968)

Warwick, Ronald and Flayhart, William. *QE2* (W. W. Norton & Co, New York, 1985)

Winter, C. W. R. *The Queen Mary* (W. W. Norton & Co, New York, 1986)

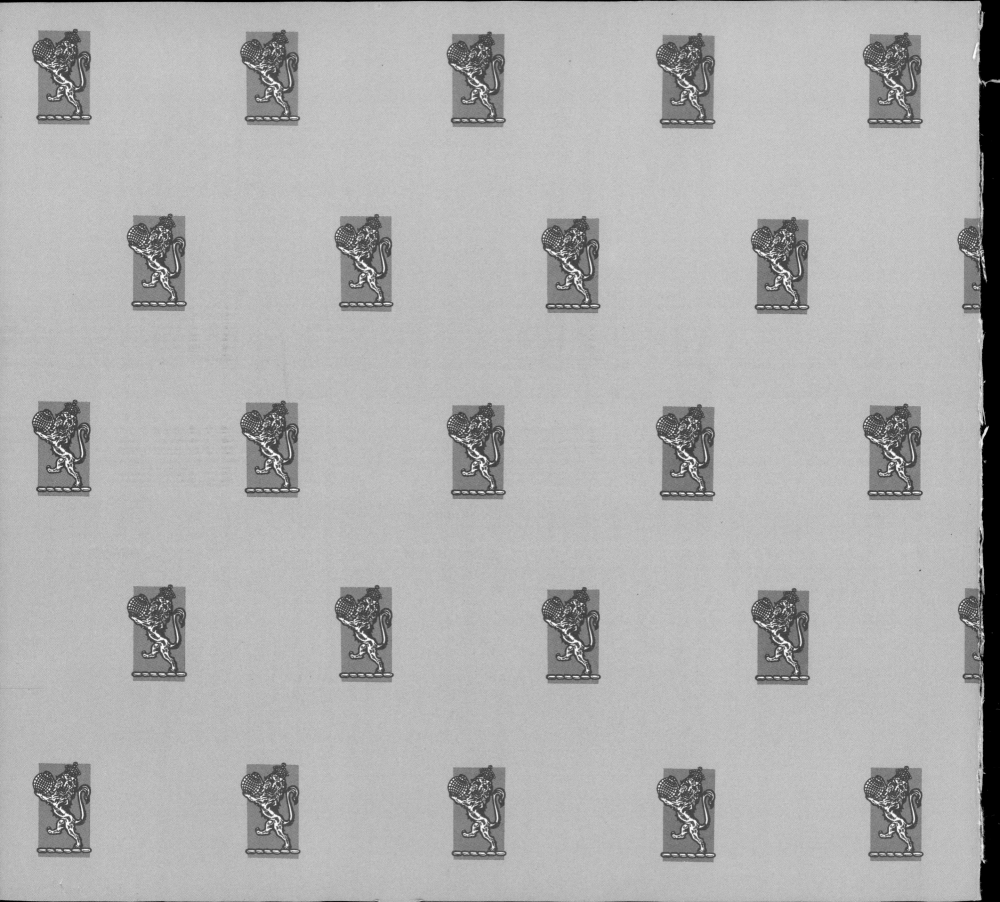